Happy Birthday Lynda
Jun 2013
~ Jim & Marilyn

About the Author

Susan Sattler is a Licensed Marriage, Family Therapist who has spent 25 years helping people move toward greater wholeness and unity in their lives. She earned her M.A. in Education at Stanford University, and her M.A. in Clinical Psychology at John F. Kennedy University. She teaches Eastern healing practices throughout the San Francisco Bay Area, and internationally for the New Century Foundation International. She lives with her husband, Gary Newman, and cat, Ink Spot, on two beautiful acres in the hills of Sonoma County, California.

For more information about Susan and her work, please visit:
www.universal-wisdom.com
thefearlesswaybook.com
The Fearless Way also has a Facebook page.

"Susan Sattler gives us an in depth account of her personal growth, and especially how the challenges of life, including cancer, were used to inspire a greater awakening. She helps us understand and accept the impermanence in the world, and a valuable exercise for dealing with it. I recommend this book to all who are interested in turning the lead in your life into gold."

—Henry Grayson, PhD
Author of *Mindful Loving* and
Use Your Body To Heal Your Mind

The Fearless Way

Mudras, Mantras, & Chemo
How Learning to Let Go Saved My Life

A Memoir by Susan Sattler

Forewords by Dwight McKee, MD
and Yuan Miao

Phoenix Century Press
P.O. Box 1792
Sausalito, CA 94966

www.phoenixcenturypress.com

The Fearless Way: Mudras, Mantras, & Chemo –
How Learning to Let Go Saved My Life
by Susan Sattler

www.thefearlesswaybook.com
www.universal-wisdom.com
www.ncfinternational.org

Forewords by Dwight McKee, MD
and Yuan Miao

Illustrations, cover and interior design by Gary Newman
www.newmango.com

Printed in the United States of America

Contents

Exercises

Foreword
by Dwight McKee, MD

This is a wonderful book, on so many levels. First, it is a very entertaining story. While reading an early draft of it, I was traveling to South Dakota to be with my wife and her 94-year-old mother, who was nearing the end of her life in an inpatient hospice in Sioux Falls. I nearly always work on my laptop computer during long flights, but on this flight, it remained under the seat in front of me, as I devoured Susan's story. I was so engrossed in the book, that when I changed planes in Minneapolis, I left my laptop on the plane—something I had never done. I was already on the next flight to Sioux Falls when I realized it. Normally I would panic—I had a great deal of work that had not been backed up—loss of it would be a huge catastrophe to my work life. However, the state of mind I found myself in, reading the story of Susan, her journey with lymphoma, her meeting and studying in the wisdom of Miao, had put my own mind into a state of calm and trust. I knew I would get the computer back, and I did—four days later.

Susan's book is also an inspiring story of one woman's healing path, a story of integrative medicine, and a story of integrative spirituality. As a board certified medical oncologist and hematologist, I can say that the lymphoma Susan had—follicular large cell lymphoma, stage III—certainly had strong potential to recur after achieving a complete remission, which now, more than 5 years on, it has not. This does not, in and of itself, constitute a miracle. But it is very, very good. In science, when we deal with one unusual healing, or a handful of them, we cannot yet be sure if it represents something new and remarkable or simply an aberration that happens every now and then. But Susan's journey, integrating the ancient wisdom of her Chinese/Tibetan teacher into her treatment, took her beyond the realm of current science.

It is my belief that each of us, when confronted with a life threatening illness, already holds within us the seeds of healing. The path to finding those seeds, nourishing them, and bringing them to fruition, is probably unique for every individual, just as our fingerprints, our DNA, and the aberrant genetic expression of every tumor that develops within us, is unique. Certainly there are principles that can be broadly applied, but it is up to each of us to discover our own unique path, our own unique combination. I think it is often a mistake for someone to try to copy the details of what another person did that resulted in their healing.

But there are some universal principles. If we are trapped in fear, and waging all out war against a disease, we won't be able to hear or sense the clues of what it is our bodies, minds, and spirits need for healing. That is why it is so wonderful that in her final draft Susan has included actual exercises, in a self-help format, that you can do yourself to quiet your mind and manage challenging emotions.

In 40-plus years of practicing medicine, and most of that time focused on cancer medicine, I have learned that healing and physical recovery are not always the same. I have known people who physically recovered, but were not healed, and conversely, those who died, and yet were profoundly healed. Susan Sattler has had the great good fortune to discover a way to experience both healing and physical recovery. Her book holds many specifics for people drawn to follow a path similar to hers. There are also many principles that apply to a variety of different healing paths.

Above all, Susan shows us how she pays attention, stays alert to her subtle messages and listens to her intuition. She seeks out the best that Western science has to offer, while spending time every day to quiet her mind, nourish her body, and to remember that everything is connected. It's a wonderful and mysterious universe that we live in—it can be terrible, and it can be enchanting. I invite you to take the ride that awaits you in these pages. You too can follow this path.

Foreword
by Yuan Miao

When ordinary people use their fingers or bodies, we call those "movements" or "postures," but when the great sages do the same thing, we call those "mudras" or "full-body mudras." Why?

When ordinary people make vocal sounds, we call those "speech," or "singing." But why do we call the sounds of the sages "mantras?"

Mudras and Mantras are not about ancient Eastern civilizations, especially not their religions; they are about consciousness or energy of consciousness, which is extremely simple and luxurious.

In order to expand and accelerate peoples' consciousness, we have to discover and redefine the purposes of the human body's activities. They are not only about survival; they also have other metaphysical potential, even including the ability for self-induced chemotherapy, which is outside our current medical modality.

* * *

同樣的十指和身體結構，為什麼普通人稱這些活動是“動作”或“姿勢”， 而偉大的聖人們的活動則被稱為“手印”或“身印”？

同樣的發聲器官，為什麼普通人的聲音稱為“語言”“唱歌”或者……　而聖人們的聲音則稱為“梵音”。

Mudra and Mantra 探索的不是有關東方古老文明更不是宗教，而是意識。 是那種極簡單有極奢侈的意識能量。

意識的擴張和提昇，是發現並重新定位人類物質身體不僅僅是為了“生存”而活動，還有許多形而上帝潛能，甚至包括現代醫療之外的自身化療……

Preface

Dear Reader—

Since you are reading this introduction, I'm making the assumption that so far you have not been daunted by the title of my book. I'm aware that Fearless is a loaded word. Is it possible to be fearless? If it is even possible, is it advisable? Am I talking about isolated moments of courage, or a pervasive way of life?

And then, there is that subtitle. If you found yourself asking, "What the heck are mudras?" you're not alone. One of the first things people ask if you mention that you are writing a book is, "What's the title?" The second thing almost everyone asks *me* is, "What are mudras?" So I was well aware that I was taking a risk using the word mudras in my title.

In fact, I spent months as I worked on the book, trying to come up with a different title: catchier, universally appealing, yes, sexier. As I swam my daily laps in the local pool, I'd try to free my mind to come up with alternatives—"Meeting Buddha on My Way to the Oncologist," stroke, breath, stroke, breath—OK, not sexier. I'm not really wired that way—quick with clever, flirtatious sound bites. A psychotherapist, I am seduced by the complexity of life: loving to make connections, diving deeper into overlapping layers, weaving interrelationships.

When I was 19 years old, I lay on the hot sand of the beach by the lake near my hometown with the first love of my life, our limbs a tangle of brown skin, suntan lotion and sweat. He smelled good, like hormonal boy, his skin tasted like salt. Ever since I was 16 we had spent our summers waterskiing, floating on our backs at night in the warm summer water of the lake, looking up at a sky alight with Midwestern stars, and fantasizing about our future together. In the winter while he was away at college I faithfully wore his old letter jacket and wrote love letters to him every night.

Lazily untangling my arms and legs, I propped myself up on one elbow. As of this year, I was at college too. "My favorite English teacher at school was telling us that there were these poets who thought we could shape our reality with our imagination! I keep thinking about that—wondering if that's possible."

He got up and absently skipped a rock across the sparkling surface of the water. "Oh, Sue, you think too much." He said it playfully, even with some affection, but in that moment some essential connection between us began to loosen and fray around the edges. He liked skimming along the calm, glassy surface; I already knew I wanted to explore the depths.

So it's no surprise that I never did find that catchy, sexy title for this book. I kept wanting to include Mudras, Mantras and Chemo, hoping you would read this subtitle and, even if you didn't know exactly what mudras were, you might swim below the surface, imagining ancient healing lineages from the Far East, maybe from China and Tibet, esoteric, mystical secrets, and synchronistic meetings with an enlightened healer. I hoped you might wonder what this could possibly have to do with chemotherapy.

So, that's a lot to expect from three words, although it's all in the book. But there is so much more to tell you: about how I grew up in a doctor's family in a small Midwestern town where I was influenced by both my family Christian lineage and the mystical power I was exposed to through experiences with the Lakota Native Americans in South Dakota;

about my past and experiences in the '60s and '70s that taught me reality is not always what we think it is; about how a suicide, a death, and a life threatening illness taught me to accept that we can't always control everything that happens; and about how, after being a spiritual seeker all of my life, I finally met an enlightened woman master who had recently come alone to the west and who changed my life by teaching me about the healing power of the Blue Pearl.

When I was diagnosed with cancer, I slid through a worm hole into a parallel universe where I explored a land of sickness and a land of healing, challenging me to reconnect with and unite all parts of myself: experimental, traditional, Eastern and Western, male and female, mystical, spiritual, emotional, psychological and scientific. Cancer and I went on a journey to find my true self.

Maybe you were drawn to my book because you or a loved one has cancer. Maybe you are a spiritual seeker. Maybe you are both. Maybe you lived through the transformational Sixties, or maybe you would just like to hear the stories of those of us who did. Maybe you love memoirs and are fascinated by the unique lives of others. Maybe you are a healer who works with the sick. And maybe, you just want the answer to the question, "What the heck are mudras?"

So here's a brief introduction. Mudras are basically hand signals (with the fingers in specific positions) that carry an energetic message. They have the potential to carry a positive or negative force. Actually we use our modern, human versions of them everyday. We give thumbs up, flash the peace sign or give someone "the finger." But there are other, sacred mudras that have been passed down as part of ancient spiritual traditions for generations. Until recently many of these were esoteric and secret, only revealed to a chosen few. It is these sacred mudras that have the power to facilitate a connection with our true inner nature—divine, perfect, infinite—the healing Source.

This is the story of my search to find my way home to this Source.

* * *

A note to readers:

I originally wrote this book as a memoir, wanting to share my healing journey, and hoping my story might help others confronted with loss. Early readers suggested that some of you might like me to share a few of the actual practices that helped me so you could practice, too. So, you will find that after some of the chapters I have offered a set of exercises for those of you who might like them. If you prefer to just read my story, feel free to skip over the exercises. If you are attracted to them, feel free to only do those that appeal to you. Selecting any set or part of a set and practicing with dedication will yield results.

1

What Is the Tether that Holds Us to Life?

June, 2004

I am standing in my office, stunned. My cell phone is sliding from my left hand, which has fallen limply to my side after my thumb mechanically hit the end button.

End.

End of call.

End of life.

The words of my client's son echo relentlessly in my mind. "We've had a family tragedy. Dad took his life last Saturday."

Took his life. Took **his** life. Took his **life**.

Time stands still the way it does during a traumatic event. Yellow light is streaming in through the wavy glass windows of my old Victorian office building. I am alone. I feel confused; a hot sensation of panic creeps up the back of my neck. I feel a strangled sob beating conscious thought to the surface.

Exactly three weeks ago, clad in his signature blue Hawaiian shirt and flip flops, Dan bounded up the stairs to this same attic office, eager to have his regular psychotherapy appointment with me before heading off for a three-week vacation in Costa Rica. "Hey, Susan, we're on track. I'm in the zone—Mr. Balance, here, ready to head out for an adventure." I must have let a fleeting look of concern cross my face, because he laughed, "Don't worry, I'm not piloting any Japanese executives, just ready to enjoy a normal vacation."

He was referring to a harrowing psychotherapy session we experienced almost a year before this, a pivotal moment in our work together. Striding into my office that day, he was agitated and talking fast. "I'm telling you, Susan, this new business as an executive pilot is going to make me millions. It's genius. I'm putting in the order for the plane this afternoon. I've been calling companies like Toyota, Microsoft and IBM all morning." His words were coming like machine gun fire, faster and faster. "Honda, Mitsubishi, Hewlett Packard, hell, they all fly all over the world. Why not me? Money, money, money."

Needing to do some reality testing, I gently confronted him, "I know you have many talents. Like we've talked about, you have the ability to learn just about anything you put your mind to. This could be something to work toward, but there would be steps to take before you launched a project like this. Do you have a pilot's license?"

There was an instant, angry flash, "You're starting to sound just like all the others. Fuck you. I don't need you or anyone else to do this. You're all jealous. I'll be making seven figures in a year. I thought you were supposed to believe in me. Fuck you." He stood up and paced around the room, his face contorted with rage. My stomach was tightening, adrenalin was coursing through my body, causing my hands to shake.

I remember feeling like I had taken a massive dose of amphetamines, and thinking, "Great, just what we need—both of our central nervous systems racing out of control." Taking a deep breath, I was trying to think fast. How could I maintain our attachment bond and still confront his grandiosity? Undoubtedly he had stopped taking his meds, such a common behavior in clients struggling with bipolar disorder. So I knew I was probably not really talking to him, I was probably talking to his unbalanced brain chemistry.

I decided to begin by attempting to repair our attachment. "I do believe in you. I certainly respect how hard you have worked in therapy. We've come so far together since that first day you bravely came to my office when you were so depressed." I was relieved that he stopped his pacing and sat back down in his chair, though he was still fidgeting, sweating and glaring at me. "I told you in that first session that it sounded like you struggled with some differences in your brain chemistry that were causing you to sometimes feel agonizing depression and sometimes elevated mood that motivated you to do things you regretted later, like the gambling which got you into debt." I locked eye contact with him, using all of my strength to transmit an energetic experience of compassion and caring, but also one of firmness and concern. Part of my mind was racing, trying to remember everything I had learned about interventions to use with people struggling with bipolar disorder.

I knew at any moment he might bolt from the room. I was banking on my bottom-line strength as a therapist—my ability to connect deeply with my clients and form strong attachment bonds with them. They usually feel a sense of safety because they experience that I am empathetic and non-judgmental, and that I honestly really do care about them. But I wondered if Dan's current unbalanced chemistry would allow him to experience or remember that.

"When we met, I told you that medication would probably help you, and after you saw Dr. Jackson you agreed to take the meds. I told you that together we would begin to explore the meaning of your emotions and figure out some new strategies to make life easier, but you would need to commit to regularly taking your medication." I knew I needed to confront him, but I was concerned he would explode. "Have you been taking your meds?"

"No, I haven't been taking them. I don't need them." But his eyes were shifting; he was looking down, momentarily uncertain.

"Dan, you know I care about you. Remember I told you I would tell you if I thought you were getting off track. You need the meds. Let's call your sister; she's been such a great support before. She can help for a few days to make sure you take the meds. We can talk about your business idea, but not until you are back on the medication. I want you to put the business plans on hold for now. How's your sleep?"

"What difference does it make? I don't need to sleep. I'm fine after two hours." The bravado and aggression were surging back.

"You know that is not a good sign. We've been here before. When you stop sleeping we know your brain chemistry is getting out of whack. This is one of those times you need to trust me. Let's call your sister."

"Fuck!" He threw a couch pillow across the room; my crystal hummingbird—a bird said to possess the ability to carry prayers directly to the gods—that hung in the window crashed to the floor in an awesome spray of tiny shards. There was a moment of silence; we were in some state of suspended animation. Suddenly he was down on the floor trying to scoop up the shattered pieces. "Oh, shit," he moaned. "I broke your bird. I'm sorry, I'm sorry. I break everything that matters."

Amazingly, my voice came out calm and steady. "You haven't broken the most important thing, Dan. You're here in my office. We still have a relationship. I still care about you. You still care about trying to heal. We're still working on this together."

There was a long, tense pause. "So, OK, OK, call my sister," he shouted as he threw down the handful of hummingbird remains. "Maybe you should call Dr. Jackson while you're at it."

There was the audible sound of my released breath. I picked up the phone, dialed, and prayed his sister Diane would answer.

"Diane, this is Susan Sattler. I'm here in my office with your brother, Dan. He tells me he hasn't been taking his medication." She and I had been here before; she knew the drill. She would come pick him up, stay at his house for a few days, be sure he took his meds and she would call Dr. Jackson or me if things deteriorated. She had such patient, enduring love for her brother.

Hanging up, I threw a watchful glance at Dan who was back up and pacing, and dialed Dr. Jackson, knowing I'd get his machine. I left a message, filling him in on the situation.

Ten minutes later Diane walked into my office and said, "What's up buddy? Here, I brought the meds and some water. Drink up," she said smiling. "Let the party begin." Watching the way she activated their sibling bond, I could see how as kids they must have always stuck together in a crisis. I had never seen him defy her. As I watched him reach for the glass and swallow the first pill, I was thinking, "Thank God for Diane."

After extracting a promise from him that he would take the meds, and from her that she would call if there were any problems, I watched Dan and Diane drive off in her Ford 150 truck. She was playfully punching him in the arm; he was gesticulating as he talked a mile a minute.

Sinking into my chair that day after watching them drive away, I was flooded with post-adrenalin exhaustion, my limbs felt like they weighed a thousand pounds. Closing my eyes I tried to clear my mind and bring my awareness back to my breath. Noticing that my heartbeat was returning to normal, I tried to relax all of my muscles. As the internal quiet stabilized, I was suddenly overwhelmed with the enormity of the responsibility I often felt as a psychotherapist.

It was not unusual for things to be difficult with Dan. He was one of my most troubled clients, but also one of my most endearing: his inner world was so raw, and underneath the intense emotion, a very young, innocent boy would often peek out, the boy who knelt over the shattered bird in my office with genuine remorse: such a perfect metaphor for him and his life.

Dan had endured a many-year struggle with severe bipolar disorder before I met him. A construction worker, smart but not particularly psychologically oriented, he tried to manage his condition by himself for many years, but ultimately, worn out by the demands of his chaotic life, Diane insisted he get professional help. At the time of the broken bird session he had been regularly seeing both Dr. Jackson, a psychiatrist, and myself for about seven months. He had been taking meds, and was even attending an education/support group for bipolar adults. He looked to me for support and insight as he tried to confront and unravel the complex web that was his life. Talking for many hours in my cozy office with the gas fireplace glowing in the background, we had repeatedly confronted and contained his manic flights into intoxicating grandiosity, and then, inevitably, the depressive downward spirals into dark despair would follow. We worked so hard to find middle ground.

Attempting to design routines to support his mental health, we set regular hours for sleeping and exercise, and tried to implement healthy nutrition and social contact—the basics. We identified, challenged, and tried to revise his negative thought patterns and belief systems, like "I always break everything that matters." Dr. Jackson monitored his medication and treated his imbalanced brain chemistry. Gradually, over the past year and a half of treatment, his moods had become less and less labile. At the time of our last appointment just before he left for Costa Rica, he was working regularly and, having finalized his divorce, he had developed a new relationship that seemed to be going well. We hadn't had any major setbacks in several months.

So today I was surprised when he didn't show up for his appointment after his vacation, since he was generally very conscientious about cancellations. I assumed his trip had thrown him off. I expected him to answer the phone, be apologetic and inquire if he could still have the remainder of his session if he came late. I did not expect, "Took his life." End of life. End of our relationship.

End of innocence for me as a therapist. I am struggling to understand what has gone wrong. In 23 years of practice I have never had a client take his life. My mind is repeating, "There must have been a way to prevent this!" a mantra framing the event, and filling me with panic.

Devastated, I wander around in a fog, operating for several days on automatic pilot. What could have happened? I can only imagine the despair that must have overtaken Dan. Maybe he stopped taking his meds. I ache for the loneliness and desperation he must have felt in the moments before actually taking his life. My heart breaks for Diane. I also have a host of professional concerns. Am I responsible? Will I be sued? Could I have prevented this somehow?

What is the tether that holds us to life? What happens when it frays around the edges, breaks loose and we are catapulted, or catapult ourselves, into the next realm?

2

Two Mantras

Soon I can't sleep or eat. Unable to concentrate, I relentlessly see images of Dan descending the stairs at his last appointment, turning to smile at me and saying, "Do you think this kind of therapy really works?"

I'm flooded with memories of other troubled clients I've treated over the years. No one has ever taken his life. Ironically, just last week I received a birth announcement from a former client, Katie, a pretty, petite young woman who suffered from debilitating depression. In her familiar handwriting that, over several years of therapy, scrawled out her pain and disbelief that life could ever be more than loneliness and despair, she wrote simply, "We are thoroughly enjoying ourselves, and Susan, I know you will be glad to hear - I'm getting a really good taste of what happiness feels like—this is it! Thank you for believing in me. It's a gift I will never forget. You saved my life."

Katie began treatment with me after being released from inpatient care where she had landed after making a suicide attempt. Having experienced severe emotional abandonment as a child, she had developed a pattern of lashing out at people she cared about when their independent needs caused her to feel terrified and lost. Of course this just drove people away from her. We worked very hard together to develop a relationship in which she could tolerate my needs as a separate person, and believe that I could still care about her even when I had an independent life. Over time she began to understand that her anger often helped her avoid her scared feelings, and she developed the courage to risk talking about them.

I stare at the new baby announcement: new life, what a satisfying outcome. I had anticipated some form of new life for Dan. I didn't expect end of life.

It's so much easier to help my more high-functioning clients who want to develop healthy communication skills, learn stress management techniques, or even explore their families of origin for clues to the disruptive patterns they are unconsciously recreating in their present lives. I love that investigation; it is sort of like being a detective. But as I try to absorb the reality of Dan's death, those sessions seem very far away.

Dragging myself across the hours of my day, I reach for the life buoy of the appointment I schedule with my mentor, the consultant for my psychotherapy practice. A PhD with years of clinical experience, she is a conscientious professional. Over the years of reviewing my cases with her, I have consistently marveled at her ability to use both her sharp, clear intellectual prowess and her equally keen intuition to help me understand my clients, and develop effective, individualized treatment plans for them.

On the day of my appointment she is wearing a stylish black fitted suit with a small triangle of polka dots showing at the neckline. Offering a warm smile, she ushers me into her office where I collapse on her suede couch. Too upset to begin, I am staring at the warm, coppery brown fabric, which usually reminds me of the earth and helps me feel grounded. Now it only seems to accentuate my sense that the ground has become liquid and is shifting underneath me. I look up to meet her steady gaze; the brown of her eyes perfectly matches the couch. She is absolutely centered and grounded, waiting for me to begin.

"I can't believe Dan took his life. I need to figure out what went wrong." My voice is shaking. I'm struggling to maintain the composure of an experienced mental health professional, while a tiny child inside me is collapsing, blindsided by life.

"Let's start at the beginning," she throws down an anchor. "What was the presenting problem? What was your treatment plan? We need to review how you carried out that plan. What were your major interventions and what was the client's response to these interventions? Who else was involved in this person's treatment? Did you consult with them? Have you documented all of this?"

Her words bounce around me eliciting scenes from the months during which Dan was in treatment which flash through my mind like a movie on fast forward.

Wearing a dirty, rumpled sweat stained Hawaiian shirt, he sits on my classy lavender-grey couch for his first appointment, head in hands, moaning, "My wife left me. She actually walked out. Can you believe it? She says I'm either up all night working on ridiculous projects or in bed for days, depressed and asleep, and I guess she's right. I don't know what's wrong with me."

I'm watching power point images flash across a screen at the continuing education refresher course I am attending:

"In Bipolar disorder there are two distinct possible presenting conditions, requiring completely different interventions." I'm furiously taking notes and placing separate case notes in the margins.

There is one scene that keeps repeating. I'm watching Dan sign the agreement, which in the end he will not keep, to call me, 911, or the suicide hotline before acting on any suicidal ideation.

My consultant and I carefully and painfully review the case. "You obviously cared about him very much," she says. "You provided excellent, responsible treatment, sought consultation, coordinated care with his other providers, and took appropriate action each time he demonstrated symptoms that concerned you."

"But he died and I was his therapist."

As I search for the key that might have prevented this outcome, she fixes me with those coppery, compassionate eyes, gives me a firm look, and says, "We can't control everything that happens."

As I ride the elevator down from her office, still in tears, I realize I am clinging to this phrase, a very different mantra from mine. For days I have been repeating, "There must have been a way to prevent this." Now I am saying her words over and over, letting their meaning slowly permeate my cells.

"We can't control everything that happens. We can't control everything that happens."

3

Meeting Yuan Miao

Stumbling out of her office and into the sunlight, I know I'm too upset to drive home. Totally preoccupied, I wander aimlessly along the streets of San Rafael, one of those small northern California towns whose history began in the 1800s with the building of a mission in what was then a colonial Mexican province. The mission and this town were both called San Raphael Arcangel, named after the Archangel Raphael, the Angel of Healing. As I pass the simple white stucco mission with arched oak door and plain cross at roof peak, I'm hoping Archangel Raphael might notice me and see *my* need for healing.

Entering the commercial section of the city, I pass head shops with drug paraphernalia of all sorts interspersed with upscale, high fashion boutiques, betraying the efforts of the town to blend its hippy past with its affluent present. Suddenly I realize I have unconsciously traced familiar steps to an eclectic spiritual bookstore, aptly named Open Secret, and I am comforted to see a large poster of the Dalai Lama, his compassionate face smiling down at me.

As I enter the doorway from the street to the store, I see an easel with a large photograph of a beautiful Asian woman. It is her eyes that first capture my attention: dark, seemingly black, they are spacious and deep, open and timeless. Drifting into them, I find myself temporarily disconnected from the distractions of the world around me. I feel peaceful, as if I am suddenly connected to something greater than our daily human existence.

A woman with a stroller jostles me as she passes, jolting me out of this oceanic connection. My sensory perceptions have somehow been exponentially enhanced, and as I look back at the poster, a red blaze of intense energy flashes before my eyes. I'm startled, never having had an experience like this before. Forcing myself to focus, I see first a hand in front of a red background with index finger touching thumb, forming a hand position I think is called a mudra. Then I realize the woman in the photograph is wearing a dynamic red Chinese jacket and her long, black hair is flowing over her shoulder. Pulling all of the disparate images back together, I see again the whole woman, totally centered and present, radiating a palpable energy field even in a photograph.

There is a poster explaining that her name is Yuan Miao, and that she has recently come to the West from China and Tibet. She will be teaching a workshop at 7:30 this very evening. It is only 1:30, but I know I am staying to meet her; I already feel a connection. It does not seem like a coincidence that I am desperate, devastated, reaching for help, and this teacher has appeared. In fact, it will turn out to be one of many "coincidences" I experience with this remarkable woman.

Relieved to have arrived here, I enter and begin wandering through the main store crammed with esoteric texts, DVDs, statues, incense, and recently released books on spiritual and new age topics of all kinds. I absently pick up some prayer beads and roll them between my fingers, look through a book entitled *The Power of Now*, and gently stroke the head of a white porcelain statue of a lovely Chinese lady. Realizing this statue is identical to one I have admired in the garden of the ashram where I have taken meditation classes, I remember someone saying she is Guan Yin, but

I don't know anything about her except that she radiates a compassionate, peaceful energy that attracts me.

Walking down a short hallway flanked with bulletin boards covered with flyers and business cards for yoga teachers, energy healers, concerts and a variety of spiritual classes, I remember the first time years ago that I wandered down this hallway, and tentatively opened the nondescript, white wooden door at the end. Like a kid finding buried treasure, I discovered that it opened into a hidden and mystical meditation room, a perfect metaphor for spiritual searching. Now, even though I know the room is here, as I open the door, I still feel that sense of delight at discovering a secret.

Sitting down cross-legged, I settle into a lengthy meditation. When my mind is finally more quiet and calm, I return to the main store where I find a book, some chai tea and a cozy overstuffed chair in a private corner where I can pass the time until the evening workshop. I can't concentrate on the book; I keep hearing my consultant's words, "You can't control everything that happens." But how do we cope when life seems to suddenly spin out of control? How do we stay anchored and sane when things seem to be flying apart all around us?

When the airliners flew into the World Trade Towers on 9/11, I spontaneously walked into the church near my office and fervently prayed for the entire world, my hands unconsciously forming the universal position of prayer. But the truth is, like many of my generation, I've moved away from my original Christian church. It's difficult to explain exactly why. I could claim disillusion with the abuses of power and control, which can occur in any organized religion, but my childhood protestant church was actually pretty non-doctrinaire. I'm still guided and comforted by the principles I learned there, but for many years I've been drawn to develop a broader spiritual perspective, which is not constrained within the boundaries of Christian dogma.

In times of crisis, I have often felt I needed more practical tools than the church seemed to offer. As I try to deal with my client's death, I feel the need for those tools now. Dozing off, entering that twilight state between waking and sleeping, I realize part of the 23rd Psalm from the Bible is going through my mind, like a song that gets stuck in your head: "The Lord is my Shepherd; I shall not want. He maketh me to lie down in green pastures; He leads me beside the still waters; He restoreth my soul." I could really use some soul restoration right now, but how exactly do I get in touch with that shepherd? Wryly, I'm thinking, "Does anyone have his email address?" How do we connect with divine guidance when we need to? I spend the rest of the afternoon trying to read as these thoughts relentlessly intrude.

At 7:30, I am back in the meditation room, seated cross-legged on an azure blue zafu (meditation cushion). The room is now filled with about twenty people waiting for the workshop to begin. Buddhas and taras (female manifestations of the bodhisattva of compassion) direct their focused, calm, mysterious stares at me from scroll paintings and statues around the room. The door opens and a blonde male Westerner, dressed in all white Indian garb, enters, leading the Chinese/Tibetan woman with the oceanic eyes. Radiating a presence of calm, grounded energy, she faces us and says nothing for a very long time. After a brief interval of discomfort because of the expectation that she should speak, the silence becomes a relief, an opportunity to let our minds quiet. Totally comfortable, she seems to rest fully in the present moment. Gradually the shifting of bodies and sense of expectation lessen, and we follow her example.

Eventually the Westerner introduces himself as Gonga and asks us to share why we have come. Many seem to already know about Yuan Miao's Yoga of Joy and talk about wanting to be in the presence of that joyful energy. I am the only one to reveal, "I am here because I am struggling in a very dark place."

Obviously speaking little English, Miao only says, "Now we will play."

Smiling, she playfully begins to pull spool after spool of colored yarn out of a large sienna-colored Chinese bag. After cutting the yarn into small pieces, she has each of us select one, instructing us, with Gonga's assistance, to just sense which color attracts us. I am immediately drawn to a pink strand, which is not usually my favorite color.

"Intuition," she says, "we must learn to trust our intuition."

I have only a moment to wonder what my intuition is telling me through my choice of the pink yarn, because settling back into the non-verbal state, she closes her eyes and we follow along into a standing meditation. Low, guttural sounds begin to emanate from her, filling the room. Ranging from low to high, melodic to discordant, the sounds are definitely unearthly.

I begin to hear a few familiar syllables like OM, AH and HUM which I recognize from mantras we chant at the ashram. Although I am not a formal member, I regularly take meditation classes there. I already know that sacred mantras are sounds - syllables and words - usually passed down through ancient lineages, which are believed to have the power to transform. I am familiar with the sense of calm and harmony I experience when I chant them. As we meditate, I listen to Yuan Miao's voice and I feel totally absorbed in the vibrations.

As we listen to the primordial healing sounds from Miao's lineage, she encourages us to move freely, following whatever our bodies feel inclined to do. Losing myself in sound and movement I have the following vision:

I'm walking in the forest and I come across an impossibly huge tube of skin, obviously shed by a snake. Then, in the distance, I see an equally gigantic diamond-backed rattlesnake slithering through the trees. He is hidden and sinister, but Miao's mantras are soothing, calming, and quieting him. For the moment he is staying in the background, sliding silently through the trees, moving seamlessly through dark and shadowy realms.

I realize Dan's suicide has called me to deeply enter into and explore these realms, but I think it will be a quick descent and return. I do not anticipate the increasing severity of the challenges I will face there. I do not yet understand that this is only the first in a series of life experiences that will call upon me to let go of my illusion of control—to transform the way I live if I want to survive. All I have to do is learn the trick of sliding out of my old skin.

The world looks different as I exit the bookstore: the stars are brighter, colors more intense. I'm the person getting into my car and the person watching me do so at the same time. I sense that a significant shift has already taken place in my consciousness.

What I don't grasp at all as I leave the workshop is that I have just embarked on a profound journey with a spiritual master whose teachings and practices will be my guide when my own tether to this realm is ravaged by cancer and threatens to break loose three years from now.

"Pulling all of the disparate images back together, I see again the whole woman, totally centered and present, radiating a palpable energy field even in a photograph."

4

Churches, Sit Ins and Sitars

At the time of this workshop, I already think of myself as more spiritual than religious. I connect religion with following a particular doctrine with organized behaviors. I think of belonging to and attending a particular church, mosque, synagogue or temple. When I think spiritual I think about a more personalized, less structured connection to divine consciousness. I think of a more pluralistic approach, combining teachings and practices from many different traditions. I think of a variety of experiences of unity: sensing a oneness with all creation during meditation; walking in nature; deeply connecting with a client telling me of a recent loss; holding a pose in a yoga class; making love.

However, I do have a religious foundation. I was raised in the 1950s and 1960s in a small town in the Midwest where most families went to church on Sundays. I pretty much knew whether each of my friends was a Catholic, Methodist, Episcopalian or Lutheran. I think there was one Jewish family in our town, but almost everyone I knew had a Christian heritage.

As a child attending Sunday school at the Congregational Church, I was comforted hearing the parables in the New Testament, sweet stories Jesus is said to have told illustrating God's love for us. I loved the one about the lost sheep. Jesus poses the question, "Suppose a shepherd has a hundred sheep and loses one of them. Does he not leave the ninety-nine in the open country and go after the lost sheep until he finds it? And when he finds it, he joyfully puts it on his shoulders and goes home. Then he calls his friends and neighbors together and says, 'Rejoice with me, I have found my lost sheep.'" As a child I always believed that no matter how lost I might be, God would somehow come looking for me.

As I got older, passing my time during the church service staring at the huge and colorful stained glass windows with pictures of Jesus holding the baby lambs, I believed the Good Samaritan would magically appear and help me if I were ever in trouble. Better yet, I fantasized about *being* the Good Samaritan, a kind of child prodigy Mother Teresa.

What I mainly remember from my childhood religious education is the definition of God: "God is love." Fortunately I was somehow spared the idea that he was an old man up in the sky, running affairs on earth. Even as a child I understood we were talking about an amorphous power or force in the universe, perhaps an "intelligence" of a sort, greater than ourselves. I remember learning that He is not a "noisy gong or a clanging cymbal," and that He is not "proud or arrogant." I was comforted by the line in the 23rd Psalm, "Yea, though I walk through the valley of the shadow of death, I fear no evil."

I was left with my youthful, innocent understanding of my Christian church. I only internalized the essence of its spiritual core: God is love. Jesus is the son of God - he has infinite love, compassion and forgiveness. We should try to emulate those qualities. Following his example, we should try to help those less fortunate than ourselves. Sometimes we have to let go of our idea of how things should be and surrender, "Thy will be done." Even if people treat you very badly, you must try to extend forgiveness—"Forgive them Father, for they know not what they do." Christ rose from the dead; transformation is possible. I had a child's understanding: simple, innocent, pure faith. These beliefs became a part of my deep inner self, my heart, and one path home to my highest potential.

Eventually going off to college in the late '60s, I went through one of my first major transformations. I arrived at school in the red wool dress my mother had sewn for me from a McCalls pattern, but by my sophomore year I was embroidering flowers and peace signs onto my hippie jeans. It was a crazy time to be in college. My memories refuse to obey chronological time. They are a chaotic mixture of gorgeous coeds in black cocktail dresses swirling mixed drinks at classic fraternity parties, oddly juxtaposed with long-haired hippies marching and chanting anti-war slogans. In the far recesses of my mind, an innocent South Dakota girl reads Wordsworth, next to her hippy self who is yelling, "Hell, no, we won't go," as the anti-war demonstration she has joined morphs into an angry mob she can't escape. Strangers are hurling rocks and bottles through plate glass windows, the sound of the shattering glass an indelible part of my college memories.

By spring quarter of my junior year my college gave up trying to conduct business as usual and offered credit equivalent to standard class credit for anyone spending the quarter educating themselves about the societal changes that were happening, and especially about the Vietnam War. My permanent college transcript bears the grade of *T* for all four classes I abandoned that quarter in favor of focusing on the massive cultural shifts underway in our nation. I have no idea what that *T* was supposed to stand for, but thinking back on it now it certainly could stand for transformation. On a campus ablaze with teach-ins and sit-ins questioning everything from our involvement in the Vietnam War to women's need to wear bras, anything connected to the "establishment" was challenged and often rejected.

Institutionalized religion came under this scrutiny. I knew from my experiences growing up that many good things could be accomplished through the organizational powers of an institution like the church: food drives, soup kitchens, and participation in large-scale world relief efforts. But I also began to be more aware that, like in any other group, it was possible for power to corrupt, and for rigid adherence to particular religious rules or beliefs to cause inflexible thinking that could even lead to intolerance or hateful acts.

By my junior year I didn't know anyone who continued to go to church on Sundays, but I knew plenty of people who were voraciously reading about Eastern spiritual traditions like Buddhism and Hinduism. One of those *T* grades I chose allowed me to deeply immerse myself in exploration of these traditions. Looking back now, I wonder, "What were we searching for?" I think we suddenly realized that our Western religious lineages were not necessarily the only paths to spiritual connection. We were searching for new ideas, new possibilities for understanding the great mystery of the universe. Already thoroughly versed in our Western Judeo-Christian heritage, we were hungry for ancient knowledge from other cultures and traditions, particularly those of the Far East. Leading our generational search, the Beatles brought us the Maharishi, the sitar, and a whole new world of spiritual practice from India.

Although I have always retained and cherished those strands of belief and comfort I internalized from my childhood Christian church, as I matured I was searching for a path with less narrow doctrine, and less orthodoxy.

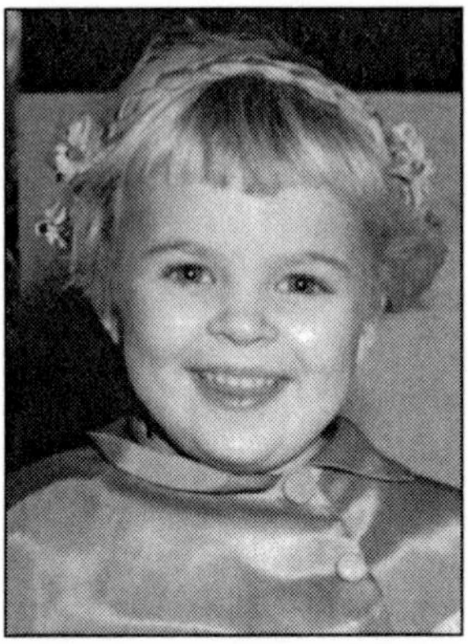

Age 4.

Going to church with Ann.

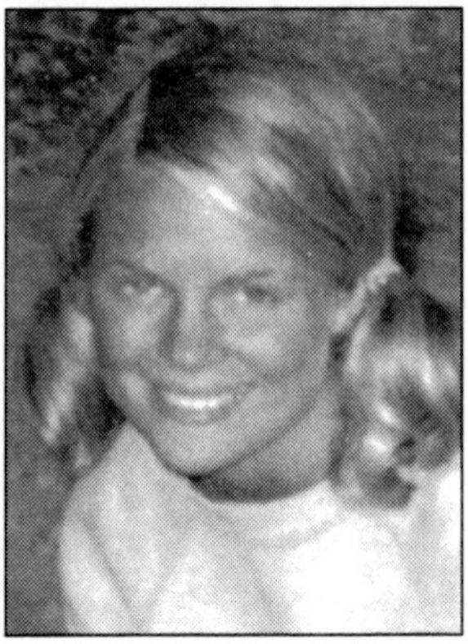

High school.

The 1970s.

5

Message from a Sioux Medicine Man

Uncertain of my next move after graduation from college in Chicago in 1971, I returned to my Midwestern roots and home state of South Dakota, where there is a deep Native American history. The land echoes with the thunderous hoof beats of Lakota Sioux riding across the plains with herds of buffalo straining to outpace them.

Growing up, I was aware of a thin veil between our present day lives and those of wise medicine men and brave Sioux leaders with names like Sitting Bull, Black Elk, and Red Cloud. I was also aware of the brutalization of their culture by mine, and the poverty, hopelessness and decline left in that wake.

Just down the highway from my family's large, two-story wood-framed house that sat on two beautiful acres, was a small cluster of tiny tarpaper shacks. My sister and I walked right past them on our way to our little rural grade school. We would often see a few dark haired, heavy-set women in worn clothes carrying water in buckets from a cistern behind the shacks. Bent over, they didn't smile; they didn't look up. I always felt overwhelmingly sad when I saw them.

When I asked my mother who lived there, she sighed, "Those are

Sioux Indians. I don't know their names."

"Why aren't they more friendly?" I asked with a seven-year-old's innocence.

"I'm sure they are very nice people, Susan. It has been hard for the Indians. A long time ago they used to be the only people living here. They had horses and loved to hunt and fish like daddy. Then white people arrived and there was a lot of fighting. Their land was taken away and for a long time they had to live in particular places called reservations. Most of the Indians still live there, but the land is not very nice. The people down the highway have apparently decided not to live on the reservation, but now they are very poor and they are probably afraid people will treat them badly."

"I wouldn't treat them badly. I think they look really sad."

My mom gave me a fond smile, "I know you would never treat them badly. Remember, 'Do unto others as you would have them do unto you,' right? They have some very wise leaders. Some of them are able to heal people like daddy can."

"You mean they are doctors?"

"A different kind of doctor than daddy, but they know how to heal people. Anyway, just smile at them when you go by and say hello, maybe it will make them feel happier."

As I grew older, I filled in the details. South Dakota matured as a state in the shadow of the massacre at Wounded Knee in 1890 where Chief Big Foot and his band of Lakota were surrounded and killed by the U.S. 7th Cavalry. When it was over, at least 150 men, women and children lay dead in the snow. Some estimate the number dead to be closer to 300.

Prior to the massacre, the United States Government had been trying to coerce the Lakota to give up their lands, especially in the Black Hills where there was thought to be gold. This was sacred land for the Lakota, and they had refused to give it up. The Lakota believe that with the massacre at Wounded Knee and the subsequent loss of their sacred land, there was a devastating loss of connection to their spirituality, breaking the sacred circle that connects the mind, body, heart and soul into a whole person. The mantra of many became, "We are broken."

Young and idealistic like my prairie minister grandfather before me, and wanting to make a difference when I arrived home after college, I applied for a job in the Indian Studies Center at the University of South Dakota, tutoring young Native American kids who were trying to make the transition from reservation life to the University.

The universe can play the trickster, however, and on a hot and humid August night, with the smell of freshly cut hay in the air, I was the one making the transition from University life back to the ancient Native American sacred practices of the reservation. Probably because I was young and expressed genuine interest in her culture, and affection for her as a person, one of my Native American students formed a strong emotional connection to me, and she invited me to participate in a sweat lodge purification and healing ceremony. Maybe there was an unconscious recognition of a spiritual connection.

"It's really powerful, Miss Sattler. The medicine man will be there. You can't get this kind of medicine from a doctor. Come with me; you'll see." In 1971, deep in the heart of the country, I was being invited into a hidden, sacred realm.

The moon was full as I clambered into the bed of Jessie's rusted, ancient pickup with two of her dark haired cousins, and we headed out of town, bouncing along dark country roads unfamiliar to me, with her German Shepherd mix, wolf look-alike, riding shotgun in the cab. As we pulled up to a rickety old wooden house with peeling paint, I could just see the sweat lodge in back.

Looking like a small igloo, the lodge consisted of a frame made of bent and crossed willow branches completely covered with old brown, grey, and black blankets, wrapped so they left a small entrance at the front, near the ground. A fire built over a pile of perfectly smooth, grey rock from the nearby Vermillion River was burning near the entrance. Shadowy figures were drawing circles and patterns in the dirt around the structure and fire.

Jessie came beside me and quietly said, "There are two words you need to say when you enter: '*Mitakuye Oyasin.*'"

"Why? What does it mean?" I whispered.

"It's been said for generations. It means 'all my relations'—that you are connected to everything, part of the circle of all things."

Joining the other young men and women, we stripped down to our underwear and formed a line to enter the sweat lodge: eight beautiful dark-skinned bodies with straight black hair and one tanned—but still white—girl with long, dark blonde, curly hair. I felt alive with a sense of curiosity and adventure. The medicine man was elderly with sagging dark skin, long silver hair, and a face whose lines and wrinkles told the story of a long life. His clear, bright eyes felt as though they pierced into my heart as he waved a tuft of burning sage and chanted over me. Crawling into the structure on hands and knees, we chanted, "*Mitakuye Oyasin,*" crawled around the perimeter to the left, sat in a circle around a shallow pit in the center filled with hot rocks from the fire, and began to sweat.

Pushing in a tin bucket of water, the medicine man entered last, closed the flap of the entrance, and we were plunged into darkness. He began to ladle water onto the rocks that hissed and spewed clouds of steam that we could feel swirling around us. In the pitch black, I began to hear low, slow chanting in a language I did not recognize.

The reality of the outside world faded, and there was only this present moment. The chanting continued, the heat increased, and I began to hear rattles and eerie sounds of wild animals near my ears, though everyone was sitting still, side-by-side; no one had entered the lodge. Small jags of light like miniature lightning bolts flashed in front of my eyes, while calm and soothing aquamarine lights floated in my peripheral vision. I felt alert with a heightened awareness, but completely calm and peaceful at the same time.

In what seemed to be the far distance, I heard the medicine man talking about the power and wisdom of the "stone people," as he referred to the river rocks, spewing their steam and emitting heat. "Yes, my children, the stone people hold all the ancient wisdom. Listen to their voices. Let the steam and heat heal and purify you. Everything in nature is sacred, a gift from the creator. Give thanks to the great spirit, Wakan Tanka, for fire from the East, air from the North, water from the South, and earth from the West."

He then began chanting, "*Wakan Tanka Tunkasila, Wakan Tanka Tunkasila, Pilamaye ye.*" Then kneeling before each of us, he asked if we needed help with anything. Disembodied, my voice floated to my ears and I heard myself saying, "I tend to be selfish and I'm not as kind to people I love as I should be."

A deep voice full of kindness, compassion, and love responded, "Little girl, you are on the right path. Don't stop. Keep going."

"Don't stop. Keep going." The mantra that is the antidote to, "We are broken." The medicine man was knitting the circle back together: offering this spiritual gift to a white girl even though it was white men who left his people broken.

As we eventually exited the sweat lodge in a daze, ran to the river, and submerged ourselves in the cool water and silver moonlight, I was unaware that this night was a preamble to powerful spiritual experiences waiting in my future.

Thirty-seven years later Yuan Miao would be my teacher and, after a particularly powerful meeting, she would say the exact same words to me.

"Don't stop. Keep going." And she would add, "I will teach you the lineage."

But on the night when I first met Yuan Miao at Open Secret Bookstore, these words were still part of future time.

6

Don't Go Back to Sleep

The morning after meeting Yuan Miao at the Open Secret Bookstore workshop, I am still dealing with my client Dan's death, and I realize I am still sad, but I no longer feel traumatized. I actually feel that a kind of transformation has taken place: my anxiety has given way to a sense of calm, as if a large, infinite space has opened to absorb my worried, anxious energy.

The workshop has been a beginning lesson in impermanence: Miao appeared, offered us an experience of expanded awareness, and now she is gone.

Having no idea if I will ever see her again, I am inspired anyway to consciously prioritize more time to place deep focus on the realm of my spirit, but not in a doctrinaire religious way. I'm not looking for external prescriptions or rules for what to believe or how to behave; I want to expand my own consciousness and experience a deeper connection with universal unity. I resolve to be more committed than I have ever been to cultivating practices designed to quiet my mind, open my heart, and help me develop courage and trust.

I decide to begin by recommitting to meditation—one of my favorite practices over the years. I have had periods of time when I have been seriously committed, meditating up to an hour or more on a daily basis, and periods when I somehow lose the motivation and stop altogether. I have experimented with many "methods," but the idea is generally the same: try to quiet the busy, thinking mind, the "monkey mind," as it is often called, so it becomes possible to connect with an expanded state of consciousness. But what does this actually mean? I find it difficult to describe in words, probably because words come from the sphere of the busy, thinking mind.

One method for meditation involves trying to connect with the "witness" mind. A question is posed, "Who is the witness?" The idea is to watch your thoughts as they arise, but rather than following them and getting caught up in an elaborate thinking process, you just notice them and then let them go, waiting for the next one to arise, as it inevitably will. It is a bit like being a sentinel on watch. You have your vantage point from which you are watching what is passing by, but you can choose whether to engage or simply watch. It is like watching storms moving across the horizon without being swept up by them. This is the witness consciousness, but who is the witness?

And that is part of the practice. The idea is to deepen your awareness and understanding of the witness and to see that all of your sensations, thoughts, feelings—everything in your experience—are a manifestation of consciousness. As you become more connected to your inner consciousness, you begin to remember and experience your connection to universal consciousness, and in that remembrance lies the possibility of knowing a state of oneness, a union with all that is and can be - universal potential.

St Francis of Assisi is credited with saying, "The one you are looking for is the one who is looking." The Sioux capture this idea with *"Mitakuye Oyasin,"* all my relations—we are connected to everything, a part of the circle of all things.

After the night of meeting Yuan Miao, in an effort to kick-start my meditation practice and heal after my client's death, I sign up for a weekend workshop at the ashram called, "The Heart of Meditation, A Course in Deepening your Practice."

Seated on our zafus in the spacious meditation hall, we listen to the Eastern sounds emanating from the harmonium played by a dark-haired woman in the front of the room. We chant a soothing and calming mantra, *Om Namo Shivaya*, until the outside world seems to recede into the background. The teacher suggests we try to align with an inner teacher, opening ourselves to the guidance which she says is always available within. She says, "Your mind has to settle into the practice. You will get only as much as you can support. You have to be content with that."

We breathe rhythmically, allowing ourselves to become aware of, and to release any tension we notice. I ease into meditation. At first my monkey mind is busy, "I really don't have time to be doing this workshop. I have Nancy, Frank and John's insurance forms to complete. I hope Toby is doing his homework. Shoot, I forgot to send in the car registration forms. I wish we had the money for a new car." And on and on, in the usual harangue of my thinking mind.

Eventually these thoughts become fewer and farther between and I begin to experience a quiet, calm, restful state. The central core of my being seems to be wide open and filled with light. I realize I feel a little bit nauseous and then I clearly see a narrow, swirling blue light that seems to be clearing out an area between my eyes. It feels gentle and kind. I have a vision of a long hallway of arches receding into infinity. I hear a voice within that says, "Reclaim your connection to joy, so it comes through your love."

As I exit the meditation, I see a fleeting image of a waif-like, small boy giving me a nostalgic look and a small wave of his hand. I feel a wave of sadness, and although I don't know exactly what this image implies, it feels significant, like a part of me saying goodbye. I sense it as something important, already known by my unconscious mind, that is just being revealed at a conscious level of awareness.

Not wanting to disrupt my meditative state after the workshop, I have reserved a room in a nearby motel rather than face the long drive home. Exhausted after the intensity of the day, I fall asleep early.

I awaken to a horrific, ear-piercing siren. It takes me a few seconds to realize the motel fire alarm is blaring. Looking at the clock I see that it is only 3:00 a.m. Pulling on my jeans, I look out my window to see the parking lot filling with half clad people as everyone exits their rooms. Cautiously opening my door, I run down the hallway, out into the night.

It turns out to be a prank by a bunch of teenagers staying in the hotel, but I realize as I am returning to my room, that there is a refrain going around in my head, repeating, "Don't go back to sleep. Don't go back to sleep." I suddenly remember that another meditation teacher of mine long ago would often intone these words at the end of our meditation sessions to remind us to continue to practice, to stay awake to our higher consciousness. I marvel at the resourcefulness of the universe: how masterful to unite teenagers with fire alarms, reminding me of this message just when I have vowed to recommit to more spiritual practice.

PRACTICE

Present Moment Awareness

Day 1:

Sit quietly for five to 10 minutes. If you have the luxury of doing this in a quiet place at home, that's great, but you can practice as opportunities present themselves throughout your day: in bed when you first wake up in the morning, while sitting in your car waiting to pick up your kids, when sitting in a waiting room before an appointment, or taking a break on a hike in nature. Close your eyes, take a deep breath and relax your muscles. Then just watch the thoughts that arise in your mind.

There is no right or wrong here; try to adopt an attitude of non-judgmental awareness. The idea is to be curious and interested in your own thinking habits. Try not to engage the thoughts at length; just notice what they are and see if there are any patterns. Are you drawn to the past, rehashing events that are over? Are you drawn to the future, thinking about events still to come? Does worry preoccupy your thoughts? Fantasy? Planning? Gratitude? When I began doing this exercise, I found it fascinating to discover how little I knew about my own thought habits.

Day 2:

Repeat the exercise from Day 1, and take a few moments to jot down in a notebook or journal the thought habits you have identified. For instance, my list might include thinking about the things I need to do on a particular day, reviewing and processing experiences and conversations I had the day before, thinking of things I need to put on my ongoing "to do" list, thinking about sessions I've had with clients in my psychotherapy practice, etc. I notice that I spend an inordinate amount of time thinking about the things

I have on my "to do" list. This doesn't leave much mental space for appreciating and integrating my present moment experiences. Having this awareness helps me make more conscious thought choices.

Day 3:

Practice a brief progressive relaxation. This will help you take a break from your habitual thoughts. Close your eyes. Breathe slowly and deeply. Begin with the top of your head and imagine all the muscles around your scalp and face softening. Let your eyelids lie quietly over your eyes. Soften all the tiny muscles surrounding your eyes and imagine your eyeballs floating effortlessly in your eye sockets. Relax your jaw. Then move your focus downward, visualizing relaxing muscle group by muscle group, until you get to your feet. Feel them solidly on the ground, connecting you to the energy of mother earth. Focus all of your attention on sensing and absorbing that energy.

Day 4:

Do the brief progressive relaxation from Day 3. Then try the following visualization: Imagine you are sitting on the banks of a river, watching it flow gently downstream. Imagine that you see things floating past you: leaves, sticks, a feather, maybe an occasional piece of man-made debris like a paper cup or a piece of old plastic. Practice noting what each object is with no judgment, and then letting it flow on down the river while you look to see the next thing that presents itself. Try to resist the temptation to think about any one object. Just note what it is and let it float out of sight.

Day 5:

Practice again, watching your own thoughts float by. Close your eyes, take a deep breath and relax your muscles. Simply notice each thought as it arises, name it ("thinking about Gary"), and then let it go, watching for what comes up next.

Day 6:

Practice this technique in a friendly encounter with another person. Relax your muscles. As the person speaks to you, notice your thoughts or emotions as they arise. Try not to judge these thoughts and emotions; just notice them, let them go, and return to a focus on what the person is trying to communicate. I find I am much more present and able to listen when I am not distracted by following a train of my own thoughts.

Day 7:

Practice this technique during a distressing event. Take a deep breath and relax your muscles. Notice any thoughts or emotions that arise, trying not to judge them. Simply notice these thoughts and emotions, and let them go. Return your focus to gathering the information that will help you respond calmly and effectively to the situation at hand.

7

South Dakota

Life races by: my psychotherapy practice is busy; my husband, Gary, finds a new job and leaves the newspaper where he has been working as a graphic designer for many years; and my son, Toby, begins high school. While I may not have gone completely "back to sleep," I have to admit that, spiritually speaking, I am dozing much of the time. I do not see or hear about Yuan Miao again for more than a year.

In August, following his freshman year, Toby (who has just turned 15) and I make our regular summer trek back to visit my parents who, at ages 87 and 91, continue to live in my childhood home in South Dakota. Still paying his dues as a designer at a new company, Gary is unable to join us; but, making it a reunion, my older sister, Ann, comes from Massachusetts with my niece, Meredith, who is now 22, and nephew, Andy, who is 25. Her husband, who runs a medical research lab at Harvard, can't come either, so it's just us sisters and our kids.

Still on California time the first morning, I sleep in and then wander down to the kitchen barefoot, in tee shirt and shorts. Ann is sitting at the kitchen table, drinking coffee, looking at an article in the New York Times she brought from home, and absently tucking strands of the practical, brunette bob she has sported for years, behind her ear. Her feet, encased in the blue plastic Crocs she typically wears at their lake house in New Hampshire, are propped up on a chair. "I'm reading about Jeanine Pirro who just announced her Republican candidacy for the Senate seat from New York. I can't imagine anyone thinks she could beat Hillary."

"Who's Jeanine Pirro?" I ask sleepily.

"Well, let me read this to you. 'Jeanine Ferris Pirro (born June 2, 1951) is a former prosecutor, judge, and elected official from the state of New York, who is currently a legal analyst and television personality…'"

She's on a roll, all neurons firing, intellect fully engaged. I'm thinking about how different we are in some ways. Definitely an intellectual, she has a mind hungry for information. Like my mother, she loves to debate and discuss politics. A National Merit Scholarship winner in high school who went on to college at Stanford University, eventually becoming a medical doctor like my dad, she was a tough academic act to follow. I was smart, but my mind has always been more drawn to psychological and philosophic inquiry, and immersion in the experience of the moment.

Staring out the tall bank of windows that span the corner of our family room, I'm watching Toby, Andy and Meredith, balancing precariously on the old, green John Deere bicycles that they have ridden here at their Grandparents' home every summer since they were grade school kids. Before that it was tricycles and strollers. They are racing around the driveway that circles the property, flashing past the dazzling colors of my mom's overflowing flower gardens. Vast expanses of green lawn that my dad has tended meticulously for 55 years, canopied by huge Midwestern shade trees, stretch out in all directions, blanketing two acres.

I'm making a half-hearted attempt to think about Jeanine Pirro, wanting to appear intellectually savvy, but really I'm thinking about my dad. In years past, before the encroaching blindness he now suffers from macular degeneration, he would have been busy the week before our arrival, carting bikes to the local "filling station" to pump up tires, repairing the tree house he built in the old mulberry tree for the grandkids when they were young, and making sure juicy red tomatoes were ready in his giant vegetable garden.

This year, as they adjust to my dad's blindness, only my mom has been collecting abandoned birds' nests she finds in the grove of pine trees she and my dad planted years ago, clipping errant dead heads in her flower gardens so they are perfect flows of color, and piling the kitchen table with books, newspaper clippings and magazine articles she knows will interest one or the other of us.

"Isn't it amazing, Ann? I know so few people who still have their family home to return to. I always feel at peace here."

She looks up from the newspaper. "I know what you mean, but it's getting more difficult for mother and dad to keep up with all this. I think we should be seriously considering that assisted living place near me in Massachusetts that I took them to see."

My stomach tightens. This is a touchy subject between us. The older sister, she tends to feel a heightened sense of responsibility. I know she has emotional attachment to this place too, but she's trying to be pragmatic, wanting to anticipate and prepare for needs that may be coming. This still feels like home to me; we moved to this house when I was a year old. I can't imagine life without it.

But that night after everyone else has gone to bed, we are back in synch, sisters drinking gin and tonics and going through boxes and boxes of old photographs in the basement. We have some sentimental moments seeing ourselves as children: holding up swimming medals we won on a relay team together, twirling our batons in our back yard circus, holding up long stringers of fish caught with my dad, and serving a horse-shoe-shaped cake to the first foal born to our beloved horse, Twinkle. But we are particularly captivated by photos of our mother: she has always had such a sense of style, whether riding our horses in blue jeans and boots or wearing a lavender ultra suede suit with unique hand hammered brass jewelry she bargained for in a Turkish market.

Her charisma shines out of the old photos that we look at one by one. Mother, squatting on the ground in her long jeans skirt, playing tic-tac-toe in the dust with Masai children in Africa. Mother, her face alight, as Chair of the State Constitutional Revision Commission for which she wrote the Bill of Rights. Mother, in a swirling dress, dancing to Big Band music and laughing with Dad in Chicago. Mother, surrounded by rapt 10-year-old girls at the Girl Scout Troop Camp she directed for many summers, holding a snake while explaining how it sheds its skin. Mother, trying to learn to water ski when we did, laughing at her awkward attempt, her skis crossed behind her, fearless and persevering even though she had just learned to swim a few years before.

But her radiance—the sense of light reflecting off a diamond whose facets radiate confidence, intelligence, sense of humor and laser-like attention in a conversation—is what is so attractive and compelling.

"Wow, what a dynamo she is," I say, shaking my head. "And what a challenge to live up to…"

"Just think of her as an inspiration," Ann says thoughtfully. "We're fortunate to have a mother who is such a great role model."

"But," I hasten to add, "the truth is she also has her working edges. Remember when we were kids how you could tell when she was really angry. She would seem sort of like a bomb about to explode, but she would just hold it all in, almost shaking she was so angry. Sometimes she seemed to be almost attacking the furniture with a dust cloth, or kind of silently storming around the kitchen. And then remember, sometimes she would even slam a pan down on the stove."

Using her, "Well now, Susan," voice that she often employed when she felt she had to take on the third parent role and defend the family, Ann says, "I think that probably only happened once or twice, but it was so dramatic you remembered it as happening more than it did."

I just give her a raised eyebrow and a smile, knowing there is no use debating.

"You have to remember the times," Ann says with more than a hint of irritation. "She was a smart, independent woman, trying to live within the confines of being a '50s wife and mother. In today's world she would have had a career of her own. That's why she became so involved in the women's movement. Remember how she served on the governor's status of women commission? That's why she was so insistent that we develop careers of our own."

"I know all that," I finally respond. "I'm not criticizing her—just reminding myself that she is a real person with real emotions."

A week later after days spent swimming at the lake, jumping off the high diving boards at the local swimming pool for old time's sake, and sitting around the kitchen table having endless conversations ranging from politics to our world travel adventures, we celebrate my dad's 91st birthday. Gathered around the dining room table with paper-cone birthday hats on our heads, we're eating the homemade chocolate cake we made earlier in the day when we were singing Beatles songs and dancing around the kitchen.

Mother is listening to Andy who is regaling her with stories of his summer as a public health volunteer in the Dominican Republic. I am mesmerized, looking at her wavy white hair framing her beautifully symmetric oval face, her elegant straight nose, attentive blue eyes.

"Every day I had to run the gauntlet down that dirt road from my family's house to where we were building the school," Andy says. "Wild turkeys roam around all the time, but there was one huge male turkey who tried to attack me every day. I mean, I was afraid he might try to *rape* me! I had to carry my whiffle ball bat."

Andy makes an unearthly noise which certainly could be a rapacious turkey on testosterone, puffs up his chest and flaps his arms, moving to embrace his grandmother with the imaginary threatening turkey wings, tickling her as he suddenly grabs her side. She is laughing so hard that tears are running down her cheeks, but she is trying to maintain grandmotherly gentle disapproval of the rape reference. Even so, her eyes are shining with pride in his adventurous spirit and delight that he shares her ability to tell a humorous story. "Oh, Andy!" is all she can manage, convulsed by her bursts of laughter, punctuating her attempts to fend off his embraces as he imitates the amorous turkey.

A woman ahead of her times, she has walked that fine line in life Ann was talking about, between maintaining her independent spirit and being sensitive to the conventions for behavior that still exist in a small mid-western town. Andy has always been able to appeal to her slightly irreverent side.

After dinner we take out the vinyl records, cheer as we discover the old turntable still works, and let Benny Goodman and his orchestra fill our house with Big Band sounds. Having loved to dance since they met in college in the '30s, my mom and dad slide easily into their own private union as they glide around the kitchen, cheeks touching, fond smiles betraying their private thoughts.

Mother was as comfortable dressing up for a social event as she was chatting with a child at a medical center in Africa.

My South Dakota childhood home.

My mom and dad, Isabel and Ted.

8

And Then Life Changed Forever

On the final day before I am to fly back to California, my mom and I are in my old bedroom. She is trying on clothes in preparation for packing to go with my dad for a four-month stay with Ann on the East Coast. I realize I am feeling quasi anxious about those visits to the assisted living place she intends to make, but I am focusing on helping my mother try on clothes and decide what to take. It is like old times when I was a teenager and we would stand together looking in that same mirror at me in a prom dress or cheerleader outfit, or her dressed in a sequined gown on her way to a dinner dance with my dad.

A neighbor knocks at the door and I go downstairs to greet him. I'm engrossed in conversation when my sister comes into the kitchen and says, "I think mother is having a medical emergency."

I go to the living room where my mother, dressed in a soft rose-colored warm-up outfit, is sitting in an armchair. My father is holding her hand and asking how she feels now. I kneel down in front of her and take her other hand.

"My face just feels numb like I just went to the dentist, and it's hard to talk well," she says. Thinking she may be having a stroke, I remind her of the hypnosis we've done in the past before she had open-heart surgery, and I suggest she try to relax and envision a safe, comfortable place where she likes to be.

"Oh, yes," she muses, "it was always this living room, looking out at these beautiful trees."

The doorbell rings and the room is suddenly filled with four paramedics who have an ambulance parked in the driveway. They stand looking carefully at her and ask the pertinent questions. She is still able to answer, but by now her leg has begun oddly jerking up and down uncontrollably.

They attach an oxygen tube to her nose. She is on a gurney coming through the kitchen where they have instructed me to clear a path for them. I can tell she is beginning to lose consciousness, but I am able to hug her, and whisper, "I love you. We will be in the car right behind you and the ambulance."

Through the windshield of the car I am watching the ambulance crawl at thirty miles an hour down the highway with neither flashing lights, nor sirens.

"Why aren't they hurrying?"

We are at the emergency room entrance and as the paramedics remove the gurney with my mother on it from the back of the ambulance, it is obvious that she is unconscious.

We are gathered around the bed in the emergency room with the ER doctor saying, "She has had a major hemorrhagic bleed into the brain stem. A bleed like this is catastrophic. We cannot do surgery in this part of the brain and it is unlikely she will survive. I'm sure you have talked about what kind of intervention you and she would like in a case like this."

We are gathered around a computer screen looking at an MRI of my mother's brain. My doctor sister seems to see the catastrophe that is there. I see only a blur of black, grey and white images. Ann turns to me, winces and shakes her head. I know this is bad; I can see she is confirming there is nothing we can do.

I am stunned and yet not totally surprised. Over the years we have had several dress rehearsals for an event like this, leaving me with the ridiculously conflicting experiences of preparation for her death and expectation of immortality. At age 69, my mother had open-heart, coronary bypass surgery when it was still a relatively new procedure, but she made a stunning recovery. Then she fought back from a severe stroke at age 79, which in a harsh quirk of fate, wiped out one of her greatest strengths, her ability to communicate. Through sheer will power and perseverance, she regained not only her ability to talk, but her quick wit and sense of humor that so often revealed not only her playful side, but also her lightening-quick mind.

I remember watching a serious young doctor carefully doing a mental status exam on her after a small, ultimately inconsequential subsequent stroke, when Bill Clinton was President. "Mrs. Sattler, do you have any idea who the President of the United States might be?" Combining her feminism, astute knowledge of politics and playful self, she said in her most patient voice, "Now let me see, I think it is a woman, and I'm quite sure her name is Hillary."

But now Ann, my dad, Andy, Meredith, Toby and I are all gathered around my unconscious mother who has been moved, oddly, to a room on the maternity floor of the hospital where I was born, 56 years earlier.

The doctor tells us she will die in "less than days." We are all stunned by the sudden enormity of what is happening. My sister and I make eye contact.

"I think mother would like to hear us reminisce about all the great memories we have of times with her," she says.

We spend the next eight hours telling stories of great times we all had with mother, grandmother, wife, Isabel. We sing all the Girls Scout songs she taught us as our Girl Scout leader.

Peace I ask of thee oh river, peace, peace, peace.
When we learn to live serenely, cares will cease.

From the hills I gather courage, visions of the days to be. Strength to lead and faith to follow, all are given unto me. Peace, I ask of the oh river, peace, peace, peace.

In a desperate moment, although it is August, we even sing all the Christmas carols and songs we can remember. "Angels we have heard on high, sweetly singing o'er the plain," somewhat strangely followed by, "Jingle bells, jingle bells, jingle all the way ..." A pastoral counselor comes and goes, infusing our vigil with a random prayer or group recitation of the 23rd Psalm. "The Lord is my shepherd, I shall not want...." We hold my mother's hands, stroke her arms, cheeks and forehead, and tell her of our love.

Eight hours later she takes a last breath and is physically dead. We stay around the body, not wanting to leave her, having some tentative belief that it takes time for a spirit to leave. Andy, ashen faced and choking back sobs, places pink roses across her breast, the ones he bought for her earlier in the day when we thought only that she would be leaving for the East Coast. The image of her lying in the hospital bed, roses in place, is locked in my brain.

End. End of life. End of my family as I have always known it. In shock, as if in a dream, I float through the memorial service and accompanying family reunion, unable to even begin to enter the depths of grief I know await me. After the service our house is filled with relatives and friends, their laughter and socializing seem so strange to me now. It's actually making me feel angry, as irrational as I know that is. Toby and Gary (who flew in immediately after hearing the news) plan to leave tomorrow morning, needing to get back to school and work.

Toby has been buried in his computer, and not particularly conversant with his cousins, aunts and uncles who have come from out of town. With some irritation, thinking this is 15-year-old self-centeredness, I demand to see what he is working on. With a click of the mouse, a photograph he has carefully created in Photoshop appears.

In the image, he is standing in front of the small, antique walnut stand with attached mirror, which has always stood in the corner of the dining room, supporting a silver tray. With his right hand, he is pouring from his grandmother's silver coffee pot. In the mirror, his reflection is holding an antique china coffee cup—one of the ones we have used for special occasions in this house all of his life—and his arm is extending through the surface of the mirror to receive what is being poured.

"Oh, Toby, it's beautiful," is all I can say, melting inside and choking back tears. This is the first time he has experienced the death of someone he loves: how poignantly he has portrayed, with his artist's exquisite sensibility, what he could never have said in words.

Receiving what is being poured.

9

The Blue Pearl

A week later, after seeing Ann and my dad off on a plane to Massachusetts, I fly back to California alone, feeling distinctly disoriented. A few days later, as I am idly staring at my computer in a daze, an email flashes onto my screen inviting me to attend The Joyful Teahouse, where something called The Blue Pearl Group will be meeting. A pink lotus blossom with a blue pearl in the center appears as part of the message and, electrified, I see the phrase, "Led by Yuan Miao."

It has been more than a year since our first meeting, and suddenly, within days of my mother's death, I am presented with the opportunity to be in her presence again. The tender, aching place that has been growing inside me since my mother's death, suddenly seems to soften around the edges. My heavy heart feels lighter.

On a hot September evening, slowly driving the old red Taurus inherited from my parents, I maneuver into the parking lot of the Mill Valley Community Center where the Joyful Teahouse is supposedly located. I flow with the crowd through a sea of traditional recreational activity, enter the building, and resolutely begin to peer into rooms, looking for the Joyful Teahouse.

Eventually I hear ethereal, harp-like music, sharply contrasting with the rhythmic beat of the Jazzercise class downstairs. Following the sound up the stairs, I enter a doorway and there is Yuan Miao, in floor length white Chinese silk, smiling at me, radiating energy and light and using a pick to play a horizontal stringed instrument. A small altar to her right has a black and white photo of a very old woman, a single red rose, a votive candle, and a small ivory-colored prayer wheel. To her left is an easel with a Tibetan tangka depicting the medicine Buddha, blue in aspect, and reputed to have healing powers. Across the wall in the back is a banner with the words, "Marin Joyful Teahouse Presents The Blue Pearl Group."

"Blue Pearl, Blue Pearl," she sings. "Love and compassion, most precious jewel." The rhythmic stomping of the Jazzercise feet downstairs immediately fades from my awareness.

Mesmerized, about twenty attendees are sitting on semi-circles of folding chairs. There are both men and women, dressed nicely as if coming straight from work. They seem to be a heterogeneous group; I notice a young couple holding their baby daughter, an older white haired woman fiddling with her silk scarf, a young Asian woman who smiles at me as I enter, and a young man with medium length, curly hair and friendship bracelets.

Sitting down, I close my eyes as we float into a meditation, and I begin to hear those same guttural sounds that led me to the vision of the snake and his huge shed skin fourteen months before. Miao is "singing" her ethereal mantras and moving around the room, sprinkling water on each of us from a Tibetan bowl. I feel a distinct shift of consciousness: that large, infinite space opens again within me and seems to be absorbing all the pain and grief over the loss of my mother that I have brought with me into the room. There is something about the mantras she chants that has this power of transformation.

Eventually Miao gives a talk in which she stresses the importance of connecting with our "beautiful, perfect essential nature," which she says is the Blue Pearl and has magical powers. One of her volunteers passes around the colorfully printed words to the Blue Pearl song, and we all sing it together. Two hours later, filled with vibrations of joy and love, we flow back out into the night where the stars glitter, impossibly bright.

Yuan Miao.

10

Connecting to the Vibration

I am magnetically drawn to attend these Blue Pearl Groups, which meet twice a month. They have become my life buoy as I try to once again confront the reality that, "We can't control everything that happens," and to reassemble life without my mother.

I have been enduring those awful moments of awakening in the morning with the vague sense something is wrong, transitioning into full remembrance that my mother is dead, and experiencing the loss of her all over again. When I was getting divorced at age 29 and had similar experiences, she was the one I would call for comfort and reassurance that it was all going to be OK. "Time will make it better. You're still young. You'll have a new love one day." She was right, I did have a new love, but I will never have another mother; the loss seems impossible to comprehend, a staggering hole in my life.

I have the ongoing instinct to reach for the phone to call and tell her that the lilies she planted in our yard just bloomed or that Toby's photograph—the one he created in her dining room with her silver coffee pot and china cup—won first place in the national Scholastic Art Awards. Who else can I call who would care like she did?

And, speaking of phones, now the weekly check in phone call is only with my dad, the pauses lingering, not punctuated by my mom's colorful stories and her sparkling laughter. I worry about how my sister and I will take care of him and still carry on our careers. We are only beginning to understand the magnitude of all mother was compensating for as his blindness progressed. They colluded in not revealing how precarious things had become—two white haired, life-long comrades in self-sufficiency, eking out the last possible seconds of independent life.

After my mother's stroke and father's worsening blindness, Ann and I used to joke that they were becoming one organism—my father could still write, take messages, speak and think clearly; my mother could see and maneuver them visually through the world. But now half of the organism is missing; we obviously need help. It is a daunting task just to find the help.

It becomes clear that my dad will never be able to live in the South Dakota house again. One day I realize I will never again run barefoot through that yard hoping to find the first empty locust shell, my faith in miracles revived by knowing a beautiful winged creature shed this constraint, flying away on newfound wings. I sit on our front step and weep: it is the staggering array of little holes I keep discovering throughout the fabric of my life that brings me to my knees.

But by some stroke of cosmic good fortune, Yuan Miao is present in my life. I have a vague sense that in her I am finding a source of the maternal sustenance I need. The Blue Pearl meetings are fun, and I always leave feeling better, more hopeful than when I arrived. Miao emphasizes connecting to our joyful, playful inner nature, something my mother did so naturally. On any particular Wednesday night, I come dragging in, carrying a load of stress from clients I've spent all day trying to help, jangled from the rush hour traffic, having just snarled at a guy who almost rear-ended me, and often missing my mom, but by the end of the evening I am glowing along with everyone else: energized, playful, yes, fully connected to the joy of being alive, having just experienced it first hand. I can barely stop myself from telling everyone I meet how much I love them. I am intrigued, what is happening at these meetings?

There are certainly quiet, respectful parts to the evening: we often meditate, hear a dharma (spiritual wisdom) talk and listen to Miao's transformative mantric "singing," but much of the evening we are active and playful. We laugh as we valiantly attempt to twine our fingers into intricate patterns called mudras. I become totally absorbed as I cross my fingers as if for good luck, touch thumb to tip of ring finger, and attempt to place tip of little finger over the knuckle of ring finger. If someone groans in exaggerated distress, someone else reminds him, "Think of it as yoga - finger yoga!" Everyone laughs.

We stand and open and close our arms in front of us like petals of a lotus. Miao's student Fay guides us, "Inhale to full expansion as the lotus opens, exhale completely as it closes. Visualize that radiant, joyful energy from the natural world is passing into mind and body from the lotus between your arms. While exhaling, visualize unhealthy, turbid qi being expelled from your body along with all sorts of unpleasantness." There is a palpable sense of release during these breath and movement exercises designed to clear challenging emotions and constrictions in the body.

We are often dancing around the room, playfully bumping into one another when chanting our newly learned sacred mantra: *Om Mani Padme Hum*. The evening is active, it is fun, and somehow it also connects me to a joyous, loving energy.

Over time, I begin to understand that Miao is offering us sacred secrets from her precious lineage, passed down from a long line of holy seekers in Tibet and China. She often emphasizes, "Feel the vibration. Connect with the vibration." This vibration she speaks of seems to be very literal. Certainly it includes a positive emotional experience, and even a positive physical sensation like one gets from listening to music, but ultimately I begin to understand that she is also talking about connecting to the vibration of a higher level of spiritual consciousness. I experienced this consciousness shift the first time I heard her mantric singing at Open Secret Bookstore. When I am connected to that vibration I feel joy and it is easy to extend love, compassion and forgiveness, even to myself. I'm drawn back to the group week after week, wanting to have that experience again and again.

But it becomes clear that Miao does not want us to be dependent on her. In the Blue Pearl meetings she is both giving us an experience of expanded awareness and teaching us the practices we need to do ourselves if we want to reside in a higher frequency of vibrational energy.

My long drives home after the groups give me an opportunity to do some thinking about two of the practices we are learning: mudras and mantras. Mantra is a pretty familiar concept to me. I generally understand that a word or phrase that we repeat over and over is a mantra, and that the more we repeat it, the more power it has. Every day we hear words and phrases like, "Right on!" "You suck!" "Yes!" "Go, go, go." "I can't do it." "I can do it."

Mudra is a less familiar word to me, but once I think of it as a way to communicate with hand signals I begin to notice that really they are just as common as mantras in our daily life. We give thumbs up or thumbs down, high five, and flash the peace sign or "the bird," depending on our mood. These are our modern, familiar mantras and mudras, but the ones Miao is teaching us are new to me and seem to be connecting me to something important, something positive, and something that might even be life changing.

One night, although it is late when I arrive home, I am wide awake and too energized to sleep so I pull out Miao's book, *Dancing on Rooftops with Dragons.* Opening the book at random, I read that her enlightened Tibetan grandmother, whose father was a high Tibetan Buddhist Rinpoche, transmitted these mantras to her from infancy. Fearful for her life after her famous Zen master husband was put to death during the Cultural Revolution in China, and having been sent herself to the countryside for "reeducation," this grandmother had to hide her spiritual abilities, so in her childhood Miao only thought she loved to sing. Much later she realized that while singing, her grandmother was transmitting her precious lineage to her.

Laying the book aside, I begin to think about my own grandmother. In her 80s, when I was still a grade-school child, she lived with us part time. She had been married to an ordained Christian minister, and she was very spiritual. Nurturing a deep connection with God, she read each day from her German Bible, played the piano by ear, and sang the familiar hymns we heard every Sunday in my Christian church. Playing with my dolls, I was often bathed in the sounds of "Praise God from whom all blessings flow...." As I turn out the light and try to fall asleep, I'm intrigued with thinking of these hymns as mantras, and that my grandmother's singing was a way the precious spiritual lineage of my ancestors was passed on to me through sound, the power of the vibration increasing over generations of repetition.

Miao's "Grandma."

My Grandma Sattler.

PRACTICE

Exercises from the Blue Pearl Group

Ideally, mudras and mantras are taught in person. In order to fully experience and understand them, it is best to study with a teacher. However, practicing mudras and mantras on your own is also powerful, and can help you achieve physical, emotional, mental and spiritual well-being. Miao stresses that in addition to placing your fingers in particular forms and chanting specific syllables, your breath, a humble, sincere attitude, focused intention, belief, and maintenance of a state of clear mind are critically important.

Mood Elevating Practice

Day 1

The Breath of Light. Sit quietly, eyes closed, with hands resting comfortably on your thighs.

Step 1: Imagine a clear light, emanating from the center of the universe and arriving at the crown of your head. As you inhale through your nose, imagine the light traveling down past the center of energy (chakra) in your brow, through the center of energy in your throat, and all the way to your heart center. As you exhale through your mouth, imagine the light traveling back up from the heart, through the throat center, the brow center, and out the crown of your head.

Step 2: On the next inhalation through your nose, imagine the light passing through brow, throat and heart centers, but continuing through the solar plexus and abdominal centers of energy, all the way to the root chakra at the base of the spine. As you exhale through your mouth, imagine the light passing back up through these centers and radiating out the crown of your head. Continue this for 7, 14 or 21 breaths.

Step 3: As you inhale through your nose continue to visualize pure, white light entering your crown and passing all the way to the base of your spine, but this time on the exhalation imagine the light radiating outward from your center, permeating every cell of your body. Continue this for 7, 14 or 21 breaths.

Day 2

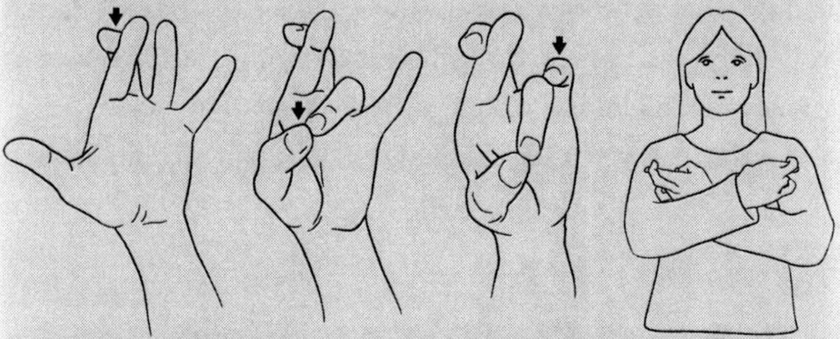

Mudra. Mood Elevating Mudra. Cross the fingers of each hand as you would to indicate good luck (middle finger over index finger.) On each hand, touch thumb nails to tips of ring fingers. On each hand, place the tip of little finger (pinky) on top of the knuckle of ring finger. Cross hands in front of your chest (still holding the mudra), relax, and practice The Breath of Light from Day 1 for 7, 14 or 21 breaths.

Day 3

Mantra: Aaaaa**.** Begin with the simple, primordial sound of **Aaaaaaaaa**. (Heard in Mama, Papa, Alleluja, Amen.) Simply breathe in through your nose using the visualization in the Breath of Light, relax, pick a single tone, and as you exhale chant Aaaaa in a long, slow, sustained tone, imagining the vibration of the sound radiating outward with the light, permeating all of your cells. Repeat for at least five minutes.

Day 4

Intention. Take time to form a very clear intention for your practice of the Mood Elevating Mudra and Mantra. Intentions should be positive - what you do want, as opposed to what you don't want. Try to form a clear statement of your intention in the present tense. For example, "I am filled with joyful, loving energy." Holding this intention in mind, form the mudra, cross your hands in front of your chest, relax and practice the Breath of Light for 7, 14 or 21 breaths.

Day 5

Putting it all together.

Sit quietly and clear your mind.

Form the Mood Elevating Mudra and cross your hands in front of your chest.

Repeat your intention silently to yourself, slowly three times.

Begin breathing, using the visualization of The Breath of Light.

When you feel ready, chant the mantra of Aaaaaaa on your exhalations, visualizing healing sound and light radiating outward, permeating all your cells.

Focus on your intention (positive, present tense) as you chant, trying to connect deeply with the energetic feeling of that intent.

Practice for at least five minutes.

Days 6 and 7

Continue to practice, lengthening the time you do the exercise as you feel comfortable. Do not be overly anxious or impatient for results. The physical forms need not be perfect. Even partially accurate forms will produce results over time. If you are serious about using the exercise to change your life, I suggest making a commitment to practice every day for 40 days.

11

Who Are You?

One night, having missed the previous Blue Pearl meeting, I arrive a little late to see Miao wearing a full-length, red Chinese silk pants suit, white prayer beads wrapped around her wrist. She is holding up a piece of white cardboard on which she has drawn a large circle with red felt pen, and then created a smiling face by adding mouth, eyes, eyebrows and hair. It is like a child's drawing, very simple and basic.

As I sit down, she holds the picture facing me and asks, "Who are you?"

Confused, not sure what we are getting at, and ultimately at a loss, I say, "I am Susan."

"NO!" she exclaims, still trying to be kind and compassionate, but clearly frustrated and a bit disappointed at how dense I can be.

She moves on to others who have wisely not missed a week and know to answer with words like, "I am loving," "I am shining," "I am joyful."

"Wow," I'm thinking, "this is certainly a happy group tonight."

Slowly I begin to understand the lesson of universal wisdom Miao is trying to impart: we are not essentially our personalities with all the vagaries of our moods and emotional/mental states. "Susan" was definitely the wrong answer! Miao has spent weeks stressing the importance of connecting to our "inner nature," which she says is our perfect, essential self at the core of our being. This is our true self, and also our highest potential, represented by the Blue Pearl. She has taught us that *Om Mani Padme Hum* means the precious jewel within the lotus. The beauty of the lotus is that it arises from mud, unstained: the mud represents our worldly lives.

What a beautiful image to see the Blue Pearl resting peacefully within that lotus. But how do we connect with and embody this perfect inner nature? I have come to enough groups now to know part of the answer: Do the practices! But what will help me over time to be resolute, to practice even when I am tired or, god forbid, BUSY!!!

Flipping the white cardboard over, Miao reveals four words scrawled in red marker across the back: COURAGE, TRUST, FAITH, SURRENDER.

Driving home, I am thinking about these four words and what I know about Miao's life. Although she was a child during the Cultural Revolution in China, she was eventually able to attend the university in Beijing, where she received a modern education. In 1984 she became interested in becoming a television reporter and director. She began working for Chinese Central Television (CCTV), and eventually became a well-known director of documentary films. She met and married a music director who also worked for CCTV, and they eventually had a beautiful daughter. She described this as being a time when she had everything in the worldly realm.

And then, tragically, her daughter, who was only nine years old, developed childhood Leukemia and died. Understandably, her trust, courage and faith were shaken to her core. Yuan Miao had to make a long, dark journey to the point of surrender: giving up her illusion of control and trusting powers greater than herself. Fortunately, she had a firm spiritual foundation to support her. Her Grandma had transmitted her lineage to her since childhood. In her book Miao says, "The external me received a modern scientific education and had a fashionable career, while the inner me was connected to the timeless spiritual universe."

Guan Yin, the bodhisattva of love and compassion, had always been her guide, although Miao didn't always recognize that this was the voice she was hearing. In 1999, she appeared to Miao and guided her to "leave everything and go to America." Speaking only a few words of English, Miao boarded a plane for Los Angeles, determined to create a foundation in the United States, one devoted to building bridges of greater cultural understanding between East and West, and enhancing the total wellness of people from all walks of life.

Every step of the way she has had to follow the teaching she is passing on to us through the Blue Pearl Group: courage, trust, faith, surrender. It is after a full year of these Blue Pearl groups, when I receive a phone call from my doctor, that I begin my own search to understand their deep meaning.

Miao.

12

Malignant Cells

I am once again standing in my office, stunned, though two and a half years have passed since my client's suicide and my first encounter with Yuan Miao. It has been a year and a half since my mother died. My cell phone is sliding from my left hand that has fallen limply to my side as I once again mechanically hit the End button. End. End of call. This time, possible end of life: my life.

My doctor's words now echo through my mind. "The cells from the needle biopsy are malignant."

Time is again standing still. The yellow light is streaming through the same wavy glass of the Victorian windows. I feel oddly calm and, weirdly, deeply connected to all life. The great equalizer has actually hunted me down, just as it eventually does every living form: ashes to ashes. I understand in a very real way, unprotected by denial, that inevitably I will not escape death, and that links me in some essential way to all of life.

Trying to absorb the magnitude of this news, I sink into the antique wicker rocker facing the window and look across the tops of roofs to the horizon. I am only 57 years old and still have a son in high school. I thought I would still have a couple or three decades to do some of those things on my future adventures list. How will Gary, who is so often described as having a "big heart," be affected by this turn of events? I know I should call him at work and relay this news, but I feel immobilized. I am acutely aware that my life as it has been has just come to a sudden halt.

Ridiculously, I find myself thinking about playing pinball at the local bowling alley with my high school boyfriend, and the odd sensation of the abrupt halt of energy flow and excitement when the Tilt sign flashes, the lights go out, and the flippers are useless. Game over. I remember that odd moment when I had to accept and assimilate the ending of the game I was so totally engaged in only milliseconds before. Whatever came next would be a totally new game.

As the initial shock begins to wear off, I feel like I have been running a race and I have unexpectedly and secretly crossed the finish line. Game over; but no one knows yet, only me. There is no new game yet, only this moment of suspended animation between games.

It feels peaceful, like that travel time when you go on vacation. You've left your work world and routine life behind, but you've not yet arrived at the new place where there will be reservations to make, cars to rent, guide books to decipher. A space between chapters opens up.

The Chinese character for the word *busy* floats behind my closed eyes.

忙

Yuan Miao has taught me that this character is made up of two characters written together. Separately, one means heart and the other means dying. The Chinese characters have evolved over several thousand years, and this one depicts that busy means heart dying.

As I sit in the sudden space following the abrupt halt of all my busyness, I have a glimmer of understanding. I am suddenly in love with the golden light streaming through the windows, the birds chirping in the trees outside, my husband, my son, my stepdaughter, my father, my sister, my niece and nephew and, in fact, all of life. I feel intoxicated with the beauty of it all: there is a huge opening of my heart.

13

Busy: Heart Dying

I am shaking, lying on my back on the cold bed of a full body scanner at the imaging center of my local hospital. A kindly attendant tucks a warm white blanket around me as if I am at some fancy upscale spa. I am about to have my heart scanned in what is called a MUGA scan, so we will have a baseline of its current functioning to compare, if necessary, with a future scan if I decide to pursue chemotherapy and suffer the possible heart damage one of the drugs can inflict.

I'm thinking how ironic it is that this scan won't show what is possibly the most fatal heart damage already done: the heart death of my busyness. I've been racing from client sessions in my psychotherapy practice, to professional continuing education seminars, to volunteer assignments in my son's classroom, to soccer games, piano lessons, scout meetings, doctor appointments, social commitments, volunteer work in the community, hastily planned "dates" with my husband, forays to my health club, the grocery store, and on and on, in a blur of frenetic activity. Even my treasured Blue Pearl meetings have been squeezed into the midst of my busy life. I am the guy on the Ed Sullivan Show twirling my poles as fast as I can, hoping not to drop any of my crazily spinning plates.

Today I have this scan sandwiched between morning and afternoon clients. I could get a lifetime achievement award for busyness.

Our culture seems to glorify busyness. Many successful corporations run twenty-four-hour shifts, people commonly juggle full-time work lives and full-time family responsibilities while trying to throw in some time for pursuing an occasional hobby, outside interest or civic contribution. When friends ask one another how they've been lately, a common reply is, "I've been really busy." It's the mantra of the Western world. While our response to that may be sympathetic, there is an implicit understanding that busy, while it may be exhausting, is somehow inherently commendable.

I always thought busy was laudable. In the external realm of accomplishments, degrees, salary, and prestige, busyness rules. My busy way of being in the world was shaped by echoes of mantras from my South Dakota pioneer ancestors: "Life is real and life is earnest!"

And it certainly was for them. As they pushed across the plains, breaking up sod and using it to build shelters that would have to keep them alive as the snow and winter winds howled across the prairie, we can bet they were busy.

"You'd better keep your nose to the grindstone," was a mantra I heard often from my hard-working, totally responsible father. My sister and I used to get the giggles saying we should both have long pointy noses by now from keeping to that grindstone. I certainly chiseled away at mine, earning my B.A. and Phi Beta Kappa at Northwestern University by the time I was 22, spending way too many hours of my young adulthood buried in the stacks of the library.

I sharpened it further with two masters degrees and a 14-year teaching career during which I implemented a girls' athletic program when Title IX came into law, requiring equal opportunity for young women and men. I began to really hone the point by launching a second professional career as psychotherapist by the time I was 35.

Obviously busy gets a lot of things accomplished, so what can be so wrong with it? Certainly ancient Chinese, with many thousand-year lineages, have great wisdom, and their characters depict busy as heart dying. Why do they depict it this way?

Out of curiosity, I look in our Webster's dictionary to see how we Westerners define busy, and I find, "1.a. engaged in action: occupied; b. being in use; 2. full of activity: bustling; 3. officious, meddling; 4. full of distracting detail."

And herein lies the dilemma for the heart of a person with a busy life. One of Webster's definitions for heart is, "one's innermost being, the central or innermost part; center." Connection to this center comes from quiet stillness; there must be room for an opening, a letting go of our frenetic activity, which is filled with "distracting detail." Then we can connect with the infinite creative power of the universe that ultimately is the origin of love, compassion, and the source of all healing. I know I need to make this connection if I want to heal, but how do I do it with the Western manta, "I'm busy, I'm busy, I'm busy," pounding in my ears?

Gliding forward on the cold bed of the scanner, I close my eyes and quiet my mind. Focusing on my beautiful heart, I vow to make room to open to its wisdom.

As I lie alone in the white coffin tube, cameras are scanning my physical heart while I am scanning my past for clues to the development of my other heart: my spiritual heart, my innermost being. I have an intuitive sense that this is the realm where my healing will take place.

At the time of this photo, I had just been diagnosed with lymphoma, but had not yet begun treatment.

14

Dear Fairfax Five

One month after I have the final diagnosis of Stage III non-Hodgkin's lymphoma, I leave my psychotherapy practice of 23 years and begin my own quest for courage and transformation as I once again struggle with the reality that, "You can't control everything that happens."

The final decision to take a leave of absence from my practice is made as Gary sits on the edge of our bed holding my hand, the slight tremor in his reminding me that he is vulnerable too. I know I should be concentrating on the decisions we need to make, but I have a vague feeling that the grim reaper might be lurking just outside the door, and that I might have a very short time to do that classic life review that comes in the face of imminent death. I'm actually finding it a very pleasant thing to do; much more enjoyable than thinking about chemotherapy and depleted bank accounts.

Letting my mind float, I'm reliving a sunny October day in 1984 that put me on the path to meeting Gary. Five of us interns who were working together at a family counseling center, trying to earn the 3,000 supervised clinical hours required for our Marriage, Family Therapist License, were sitting at an outdoor café having lunch. Nancy suddenly leaned forward and conspiratorially said, "I've got an idea to propose. You all know I've been putting personal ads in the paper and dating some men that way, but it creeps me out to be meeting strange men alone. So ... I was thinking, we're all single, how about if we do a group ad for a dinner party with the five of us, and five new men? It would be fun, and it would optimize all of our chances of meeting someone we like."

That was how the Pacific Sun, a hip, local newspaper in Marin County, leading the way in the early days of meeting through personal ads, came to print the following ad on October 12, 1984:

> *5 prof women, 34-36 attrac, slim, intell & fun, seek 5 non-smoking, friendly men w/similar qualities to create a memorable evening. We'll cook (this time). Only descriptive, thoughtful responses considered.*

And then the inundation of letters began to arrive—58 of them—long, mostly thoughtful responses from men wanting to be included in our dinner party.

> *Dear Fairfax Five,*
>
> *This is a strange letter for me to write. Seems a little like a resume or a job application - trying to find the balance between bragging and modesty. But here goes.*
>
> *I would like to be invited to dinner in your collective home. Since I doubt you'd invite just any bozo who writes you, you'll want a pretty clear idea of who I am. Well, I am Gary Newman. 5'10", 145 pounds, 37 years, brown hair, full beard. I'm athletic in that I run regularly (but not fanatically) as well as back pack, bicycle, swim and cross country ski. (I'm checking out the Sierra next weekend.) A non-smoker, I'm intelligent, politically aware, feminist-aligned, and have a good sense of humor - I don't take*

myself too seriously. I like classical and contemporary music, hiking at night under the moon, and ice cream. I'm a member of Desert Survivors—a conservationist group in the East Bay that sponsors good things and is considerably smaller and less stuffy than the Sierra Club, and has more fun. The jobs I've had include chemist, entomologist, high school teacher, spy, and cartographer. But what I am is an artist. I'm visually oriented; I see things. My art tends to the surreal –ink drawings and air brush. For the past seven years I've made my living doing art commercially. In partnership with two women, I own a design studio in San Francisco. We do all right, and have a good time.

So, how about it? Want to have dinner with me? I won't talk about politics unless you start it. But - just in case I'm not one of the chosen—if you haven't decided who to vote for yet, I beg you to vote for whoever will not invade Nicaragua. If you want to know why, call me.

Sincerely,

Gary Newman

Sitting next to him at dinner, I was on a roll, "So how about Sierraville? Have you ever cross-country skied around there? I know a great place that has rustic little cabins and an old fashioned outdoor hot pool. After skiing you can sit in the hot water and let snow flakes fall on your face."

Giving me what my friend refers to as 'full frontal attention,' he held his own. "No, I've never been there, but it sounds great. I like Sonora Pass myself. There's a meadow that's a perfect spring skiing spot."

I felt an instant recognition, like I had rediscovered an old friend. That night I slid into bed thinking, "So, Gary, here you are; you finally showed up." I don't even remember anything about the other four men.

The next weekend we were hiking five miles up a slippery waterfall trail on Mount Tamalpais. The following weekend we hiked the length of Limantour Beach, built a fire, drank hot tea he brought in a thermos, and watched a coyote skulk around us in the gathering darkness. We spent the winter skiing, watching movies entwined in each others arms, hiking in the rain and at night under the moon, and yes, eating ice cream.

In May as we were trying to say good night so he could drive the half hour back to his home, he looked very serious and said, "I don't want to be away from you. I think we should figure out a way to live together." In June we hung his surrealistic, air brushed art on the wall of my house, placed his skis and back pack next to mine in the tool shed, and raced each other for what was now "our" bed.

But now, 23 years later, here we are in that same bed that once held a beginning, facing a possible ending. Our held hands form a mudra, communicating trust, saying, "We are in this together." I know Gary's main concern is losing me, but there are also serious financial implications if I have no income.

"You can't keep seeing clients, Susan, it will be too stressful for you. Remember what the oncologist said when you asked him about working? He said that it was his understanding that part of the job of a therapist is to be available, a steady, predictable presence, and that it was unlikely you could be that during treatment. Remember he said you might have good days when you could work, but there would be many days you couldn't and that would probably disrupt the continuity of treatment for your clients. You have to let go. I don't know how we will make up for your lost income, but we will figure it out. The only important thing is your health."

I feel confused. Usually supremely organized, I have always been able to look ahead and figure out where I want to be and what steps are required to arrive there. I have literally banked on control. Now, facing the cancer diagnosis, it seems I need to let go of everything that has been in place for many years and open to the unknown. As I sit holding Gary's hand, Miao's Eastern lineage whispers "surrender" and weaves itself around the Western mantra, "Thy will be done."

Three days later I am standing in the doorway of our local post office, looking at the line ahead of me. These people presumably are going about their daily lives, keeping things flowing, staying on course. They are paying their bills, mailing the requisite birthday card to grandma, sending the corporate business package to company headquarters, or perhaps even mailing out a resumé. I am about to dismantle my life. Clutched in my hands are the letters to all of my clients explaining my illness, outlining my "leave of absence" and offering them names and phone numbers of other therapists they could see in my absence.

I believe I will soon return to my practice, that this is only a brief blip before I will be back in my tan leather therapist's chair working exactly as I did last week. However, some deep part of me also knows a much larger transformation is underway, because I notice the quality of the light changing as I open my hand and watch the envelopes drop through the metal outgoing-mail slot.

Things feel surreal; I feel distinctly disoriented. This is the first time in 34 years that I have not been working, and usually in a responsible, professional job. This will also be the first time in my life I do not have a plan. I feel giddy. I feel irresponsible. I feel free. I feel elated. I have to remind myself that I also have cancer, that it is only this reality which has been powerful enough to give me permission to stop: stop pushing, stop planning, stop controlling and micro-managing outcomes on every front.

1985, a few months after Gary and I met.

1989.

15

Medical Doctors and Ouija Boards

But old patterns die hard. My cancer is aggressive and I have to decide on a course of treatment quickly. Throwing myself into an attempted crash course in oncology, I Google frantically into the wee hours of each morning. The more overwhelmed I feel, the busier I become, searching for statistics on efficacy of treatments and rates of survival. I'm reading about double-blind studies with large numbers of people that can be replicated. Surely, if I just marshal enough knowledge, I can determine the exact treatment that will save my life. I may have surrendered in the realm of my psychotherapy practice, but I have not even begun to explore what surrender means in terms of my cancer.

I come from a Western medical background. My M.D. father was an internist, widely respected for his skill at diagnosis, but also for his kind and healing bedside manner. When I was a child he actually made house calls in the middle of the night. I remember standing shivering in my nightgown and bare feet, having been awakened by the phone, and watching him carefully checking his little black bag for syringes and vials of mysterious medicines. If he saw me, he would take the time to give me a hug, and with a smile say our familiar bedtime line, "Night, night, sleep tight, don't let the bedbugs bite!" Standing in the dark at the dining room window, I would watch the tail lights disappear as he drove the family Ford down our rural highway into the night, hoping to alleviate someone's suffering, and modeling that loving kindness and deep compassion are the way to relate to others.

My only sibling, Ann, became an adolescent medicine specialist and married a pediatric gastroenterologist who runs a research lab at Harvard. Trained in Western medical science, all three believe primarily in scientific proof: double-blind studies, results from studies with large numbers of people which can be replicated, and the safety and efficacy of painstakingly developed "standard of care" treatment. Indoctrinated in Western medicine and well educated from a young age, I would never totally reject that position; however, there has always been a part of me drawn to those realms beyond hard science.

My one near arrest happened when my best friend in high school convinced about twenty of us to take a Ouija board to the local cemetery one night to see if it would behave differently there. As the captain of our cheerleading squad, she had excellent powers of persuasion. Word spread through whispers at lockers and notes passed in study hall, and at 11:00 p.m., a group which included the junior class president, the captain of the debate squad, all the cheerleaders, honor students, near drop-outs, jocks, non-jocks, and probably even those we referred to as "hoods" in those days, all parked our borrowed parents' cars along a country cornfield and streamed past the grave markers of our ancestors to the heart of the cemetery.

The Ouija board consisted of a somewhat slick, thin board with letters of the alphabet arranged in an arc across the top. There was a separate free-floating, heart shaped wooden piece about four inches across, which several people lightly touched with the tips of their fingers, while concentrating on connecting to the spirit world. The wooden piece appeared to move across the board under its own direction towards letters, spelling out words.

Wanting to believe, we were totally absorbed in watching the seemingly supernatural movements of the heart-shaped piece on the Ouija board while the local police, alerted by an abnormal number of cars at the cemetery that night, trudged past the tombstones bearing names of both their forebears and ours, to confront us.

The ghosts of our pioneer ancestors might not have been deliberately spelling out messages to us on the Ouija board that night, but nonetheless many of us heard the whispers from mystical realms, reminding us of the mystery of the unknown and the seemingly undeniable possibility of miracles.

16

Exploring the Outer Edges

As an English Literature major in college, I was fascinated with the Romantic poets like Blake, Coleridge, Wordsworth, Byron, Shelley and Keats who described transcendence into experiences of immortality through merging with nature. In his famous poem, "Ode on Intimations of Immortality," Wordsworth explored his idea that it is easier for children than for adults to experience the divine within nature.

There was a time when meadow, grove, and stream,
The earth, and every common sight,
To me did seem
Apparelled in celestial light.

As he searches for an explanation, Wordsworth ventures into mystical territory, hinting at the Platonic idea of pre-existence in which the soul is believed to have existed before the body, resulting in humans' having vague memories of a divine state that existed before our worldly life: intimations of immortality.

Our birth is but a sleep and a forgetting:
The Soul that rises with us, our life's Star,

Hath had elsewhere its setting,
And cometh from afar:
Not in entire forgetfulness,
And not in utter nakedness,
But trailing clouds of glory do we come
From God, who is our home:
Heaven lies about us in our infancy!

The Romantic poets believed we must constantly search for a reality deeper than convention and tradition reveal.

I remember the electric sensation that went up my spine weeks as I sat in a stuffy, overheated classroom and heard my professor point out that classical Romanticism had a revolutionary energy at its core. "This revolutionary force consciously transformed both the theory and practice of poetry and all the other arts," he said. "It also transformed the way we see the world. The imagination came to be regarded as the supreme faculty of the mind." Up until this time, there had been general agreement, at least in Europe, on the supremacy of Reason.

I couldn't help myself, I said right out loud, "The imagination was believed to be the 'supreme faculty of the mind'? Oh, my god, I have found my people." The professor locked eye contact with me, intending a frown—spontaneous outbursts were not encouraged in formal class. But a huge grin spread across his face: he knew he had a kindred spirit on the line.

That night, back in the sorority house from which I later deactivated in an act of '60s idealism, my roommate and I were soaking a towel with Chanel #5 and stuffing it to cover the crack under our door. We had discovered we could then light up a joint undetected, kick back and indulge ourselves in philosophical exchange.

I was intense, "Maryanne, it's so far out! The Romantics believed we actually shape our reality with our imagination, sort of a force like the creative powers of nature, or even 'god.' Not only is it how we create art and perceive reality, it's the way we create reality: we are co-creators!"

I'm sure she must have said something like, "Far out, man," and it was far out for me. I loved the idea that "reality" could be fluid and changeable, that we might have the power to actually influence it. Of course, at the time I had no idea that one day that belief might actually help save my life.

But it was not only in my college classes that I was drawn to experimentation and new possibilities. Throughout the late '60s and early '70s, I continued to explore Eastern spiritual traditions, meditation, yoga, and rode along in spirit with the Beatles, Timothy Leary and Ken Kesey on "Magical Mystery Tours" and Merry Prankster-like adventures.

In the summer of 1969, my sister, her radical-intellectual boy friend (who was heavily influenced at the time by Che Guevara), my hippy college roommate and I spent a month driving to the tip of the Yucatan Peninsula in Mexico. Like others of our generation, we were seeking to expand our horizons by immersing ourselves in another culture with different ways of perceiving the world.

We ate brown rice cakes until they molded in their plastic bags (the boyfriend made them and brought them along, convinced we should try to live as cheaply as Che's guerilla fighters), camped in deserted construction lots, viewed staggering collections of Mesoamerican art and artifacts, and experienced the mystical power of ancient spirits from the tops of Mayan pyramids.

But my seeking was not confined to spirituality. My generation was experimenting with letting go in every arena. Taking the motto of the time, "Question authority," to heart, we were questioning our parents, our teachers and even our government. We were part of a cultural movement that encouraged letting go, breaking out of social convention and conformity, opening to possibility, and taking a chance.

Six months after our trip to the Yucatan, energized by the spirit of the times, my same college roommate and I hitch-hiked 500 miles from

Chicago to the University of South Dakota in the middle of February. It was 1970; we were hungry for adventure and lulled into complacency about the weather by an intoxicating false spring.

Part of the message of our generation seemed to be, "Don't be afraid, occasionally let life be uncontrolled—an adventure." John Lennon's wisdom reverberated in our collective unconscious. "One thing I can tell you is you've got to be free."

And yes, as a child of the times, I experimented with mind-altering drugs. Like many of my generation, I smoked pot. Eventually I tried magic mushrooms and then the synthetic version, psilocybin. I also tried mescaline, which in its natural state comes from the peyote cactus. Psilocybin mushrooms and peyote have been used for spiritual purposes in traditional ceremonies in Mexico and South America for generations; but my experimentation at the time was not exactly spiritual. It came closer to the Romantic poets' idea of longing to see things with a fresh perspective. One amazing thing about psychedelics is that they can allow one to experience something qualitatively different from what we generally agree to be reality.

My perception of reality changed permanently the night I took acid. I was about to set a glass on a table when I realized the table no longer appeared solid. It seemed as if I could see all the individual atoms with spaces in between so it actually just looked like a more dense collection of molecules, floating in space, sort of like a cloud. During this time, I began to understand that all form is a manifestation of density of energy. The human body is a dense energetic form, but all form can become less dense and dissolve into formlessness, like ice to water to steam, and the formless can come into form. What we think of as reality is ever shifting, illusory, and impermanent.

After college, I longed to go to California, the mecca at the time for anyone interested in experimentation. I was anti-war and a full-fledged flower child; I wanted to push the edges and find the pulse of my generation.

Dreaming of going west, I braided daisies into my long hair, turned up the volume full blast on my JVC stereo speakers, and sang, "If you're going to San Francisco, you'd better wear some flowers in your hair."

In 1971, just as I finished my stint at the Indian Studies Center in South Dakota, I got my chance to join my generational tribe in California when I pulled an envelope from my mailbox with the return address for Stanford University. A new chapter in my life began as I read that I had been accepted as a graduate student in their Master of Arts in Teaching Program. Two weeks later, with flowers in my hair, I was headed west on I-80 in my tiny Ford Falcon.

Like other universities across the country at that time, Stanford was alive with innovation and I was able to fully indulge my appetite for unexplored frontiers. My teaching assignment for the year was in an experimental high school program stressing a holistic, interdisciplinary approach. Because the course was an attempt at integrating the science and English curriculum, it was given the somewhat dubious name of "Scilish." It took about two days for our cynical teenagers to demean it by referring to it as the silage class. Despite themselves, I think they experienced a greater interest in their biology class because in English class we were reading *Fantastic Voyage* by Isaac Asimov in which four people are miniaturized and sent by tiny atomic sub on a mission through the human body to destroy a blood clot in a carotid artery.

Longing for more of a balance between mind and body than I experienced in graduate school, I was thrilled to land a job right after graduation in a small, rural, California public high school right on the coast, teaching both English and physical education. After school I would jump into my blue Mustang and in 10 minutes I could be jogging down a pristine beach, sand dunes to my left, blue waves of the Pacific Ocean rolling in on my right: plenty of opportunity for merging with nature.

Much later, after 14 years of teaching high school, fueled by a growing awareness of my deep longing to connect with whatever lay beyond the realm of the conscious mind, and still living in California, I eventually found my way to a study of psychology and psychotherapy, hardly the realms of hard science. I decided to return to school and work on my master's degree.

Within the clinical psychology program, I was especially drawn to Carl Jung, a Swiss psychiatrist who emphasized understanding the psyche through exploring the worlds of dreams, art, mythology, religion and philosophy. This led to my fascination with the realm of the unconscious, dream work, hypnosis, and, out there on the fringes, I dabbled with the I Ching, Tarot cards, and receiving intuitive readings. The potential untapped power of our expanded consciousness intrigued and called to me.

But unfortunately because of these interests, I sometimes felt separate from my family of origin, which was well-populated with those Western-trained medical doctors who relied on, trusted and respected things that had been scientifically proven. Over the years many family discussions were constrained when someone made the authoritative declaration, "There's no scientific proof of that." It seemed that scientific experiment was required to either bring an idea into the fold of "proven" and therefore respectable, or not proven, therefore not respectable.

I found it difficult to stand up to this kind of authority. I was fearful of being judged. It wasn't that I disagreed with the results of carefully crafted scientific studies. In fact, I have the greatest respect for the extensive knowledge of Western science. But I am also aware that it has its limitations.

I believe that in our collective human experience there is much of value that hasn't been scientifically validated. One of the things that always appealed to me about Eastern mystic traditions was their appreciation for direct experience. But in my family, when what I offered were personal experiences or experiences of others, without scientific proof, I sensed skepticism and sometimes felt the not-so-thinly-disguised negative judgment about practices, beliefs and ideas that were considered too "alternative."

During this time, I consulted with a well-known woman who did intuitive readings in Marin County. One of the first images she described "seeing" was of me as a young child in a huge schoolyard swing. At first I appeared to be happy and free, swinging higher and higher, but then it became apparent that I was frustrated and quite sad because I was constrained by the structure of the apparatus and could only go as high as the chains allowed.

I didn't bring my beautiful Tarot deck home, and we didn't sit around my parents' kitchen table throwing the *I Ching*. I could have introduced these things, but I felt they would make everyone uncomfortable. Worse yet, I feared they would be responded to as silly parlor games, not the beautiful, mystical pathways to deeper self-understanding that I had come to love.

Over the years as I struggled to straddle these two worlds, I often thought of two kinds of horses I witnessed growing up in South Dakota. The ones we raised and then used for riding had been tamed. Their behavior became predictable, based on a number of riding "experiments." There was safety in a horse like this, and safety is a good thing if you are riding a horse. But then there were the wild mustangs out on the range, unpredictable and free, running with manes and tails flying in the wind, filling us with the excitement and awe of unexplored potential and possibility.

17

Deciding How to Heal

Now, many years later, confronted with a life threatening condition, I have to decide how to go about healing myself. I have always gravitated toward the intuitive, the mysterious, but what do I really believe in? The stakes are not small; my life may hang in the balance. Do I throw my lot in with the safety of science and reason, or the power of the imagination to co-create reality?

I am now connected to two very different guides: my Western, Stanford University-trained oncologist and my Chinese/Tibetan teacher, influenced by her *Vajrayana* Tibetan Buddhist grandmother and her Zen master grandfather. I am also guided by three *spiritual* lineages: Western through my grandfather and grandmother, Eastern through Miao's Grandma, and Native American from the Great Spirit of the land where I was born: modern/ancient, East/West, female/male.

As I sit on a black swivel stool across from Gary in a small medical office decorated in the requisite "healing colors" of peach and light blue-green, my white-coated oncologist is outlining a course of treatment. "The standard of care treatment for non-Hodgkin's lymphoma has been the same for many years now. It has been thoroughly researched through clinical trials and major follow-up studies," he tries to reassure me. "You will undergo five to six months of chemotherapy, using five different major, toxic drugs. You will also receive a newer, monoclonal antibody called Rituxan." I'm hoping Gary is paying attention; my mind is wandering.

As I gaze at the blood pressure cuff hanging on the wall, trying to force myself to concentrate on his words, my hands are unconsciously forming the mudra for regulating blood pressure that Yuan Miao taught at last week's class. Unsolicited, *Om Mani Padme Hum* is repeating over and over in my mind, reminding me of the precious jewel within the lotus. I'm thinking about the other esoteric breathing and movement practices we've been doing to bring our energetic vibration into a healthy alignment with that universal source of love, compassion, joy and ultimate healing. How do I reconcile such disparate parts of who I am? I'm suddenly remembering a second visit I made many years ago to the woman who did intuitive readings. I returned to see her just out of curiosity, since she had been so insightful initially with her image of me in the swing. During this second visit she saw an image of me holding a baby bird with a broken wing in my hand. As I held the bird, the wing healed and the bird was able to fly away. At the time I did not understand the image.

Now I'm wondering, "What is the source within me that will allow the bones of the baby bird to heal?"

Back home, sitting on my zafu with golden sunlight pouring through our floor to ceiling living room windows, I look out at the few red leaves still clinging to the Japanese maple by the front door, still stunned that I have cancer and overwhelmed by how my life has changed. I meditate on the apparent schism in my basic beliefs. Do I trust Western medicine to cure me, or the healing power of the Blue Pearl? Is my safety in those double-blind studies or in thousand-year lineages of wisdom healing from Tibet and China? What healing medicine might still vibrate within me from the prayers I recited and the hymns I sang in my Christian church, or from the medicine man's chanting in his beautiful Lakota tongue as we sat together on our shared sacred land in South Dakota.

Slowly, the potential for all parts of my life experience to come together in beautiful synergy dawns on me: working together, all these healing paths may be more powerful than one alone. The universe is offering me the ultimate possibility for integration. Perhaps my opportunity has finally arrived to abandon the constraints of the swing and take flight with my own fledgling wings.

With this realization the design of my treatment is suddenly clear; it will be a blend of all parts of me: experimental and traditional, Eastern and Western, male and female, mystical, spiritual, emotional, psychological, and scientific. I have faith that all these aspects have the power to heal, and it will be that faith which acts as the catalyst.

Slipping into meditation, I see an image of jagged pieces of a puzzle in black and white floating randomly in space, like so many sky divers released from a plane all at once. As I watch they float together and with the joining of the final piece they come together to make a whole.

I have always thought of myself as strong, independent, and to a certain extent self-sufficient, but I also experience myself as a small part of a much larger whole. There is great power in collective intention, compassion and love. I know it is time to open to that collective energy, but I need to decide how I want to do that. Gary suggests I do a blog, but there's no controlling who has access to a blog. I want to inform my friends that I have cancer, but I also want to enlist their help energetically. I have an intuitive sense that I need to carefully select those I ask to help in my healing journey.

Lingering on my meditation cushion, I begin to think of the many deep and intimate friendships I have had the good fortune to develop with rare and wonderful people. Some have come into my life recently, but many are people I met in other eras of my life, our relationships deepening and enduring over years and even decades.

I imagine Judd, calmly smiling at an overactive ADHD child in his behavioral medicine practice in Minnesota—our mothers were pregnant at the same time, we grew up together in South Dakota, attending each other's birthday parties and even going to the same college.

I met my friend Nancy by chance on the street near my home when we were pregnant, and then we were in the same hospital when our boys were born five days apart. She had returned to the hospital with a jaundiced baby when my son was born on her birthday—she brought a rose to my room. Every Tuesday afternoon for seven years we watched our boys play in plastic pools, dig holes in the sand at the beach and run through sprinklers in backyard lawns during our mom and kids' playgroup. We've stayed close friends even though our boys have long since gone their separate ways.

Reefa was a dear friend of my mother's, one of my many hometown surrogate mothers. Her son Pete, a good friend of mine in high school, died more than 20 years ago of non-Hodgkins lymphoma. Reefa and I have always stayed in touch.

I recently saw Priscilla, my hitchhiking buddy, now a photojournalist in San Diego, at a sorority reunion. Even though we both deactivated back in hippy days, our former sorority sisters all said, "Come anyway, we want to see you, all that was long ago and our friendships trump any sorority rules,"—a testament to their true depth, dissolving any stereotype of sorority shallowness. Some of them will also receive my news.

Marg and I spent a Fellini-like night in a motel in Sacramento one October 31st, the night before we took our Marriage Family Therapist boards. As we stumbled, bleary-eyed, into the hallway, taking breaks from our frantic last minute cramming, devils and witches and deformed monsters ran past us, jumping at us, making strange noises, on their way to and from the Halloween party in the cocktail lounge, becoming more and more outrageous as the alcohol flowed.

By the time I move from living room to bedroom, I realize there are probably at least 50 people I want to include. (And now, my new-found reader friends, you too are included.) Snuggling into my bed with my laptop, white comforter enfolding me like a cloud, I begin to write the first of my cancer journey emails. I realize that ceasing all my busyness has created a space for not only self-reflection, but also for the creative expression of my thoughts in written words that I can share with others. As this creative process begins, I'm amazed that I actually feel an immediate stimulation of my life force, a sense of energy and excitement; connecting to my creativity is connecting me to the healing source.

18

A Tiny Prayer to Father Time

From: **Susan Sattler**
Date: **Feb. 1, 2007 10:17 PM**
Subject: **Susan Sattler facing big challenge**

To all my dear friends,

I am sorry to communicate the following serious and deeply personal news in the form of an email.

I have just been diagnosed with non-Hodgkins lymphoma: yes, that's cancer. We're awaiting a final pathology report from Stanford on a lymph node they removed Monday which will help refine the final exact treatment protocol. Treatment must achieve complete eradication of every malignant lymphocyte; I must achieve what they call CR, complete response, or the prognosis is not good. To that end I will be given an aggressive course of chemotherapy over the next five months. If I have not achieved CR by then I will have a bone marrow and stem cell transplant using my own blood. If I can achieve CR and not have a relapse, my doctor says I have a chance for prognosis of normal life expectancy.

We're also still waiting for the results of a bone marrow biopsy that I had done last week (which, incidentally, hurts like hell) that will tell us if the cancer is in the bone marrow or fully contained in the lymph nodes. We do know that this is a cancer of the lymphatic system, it has not spread here from some other primary site, no other organs are involved, obviously a good thing.

I will be taking a leave of absence from my psychology practice during the treatment that will begin soon after we have the final pathology report from Stanford, which should be early next week.

So, for those of you who want to hear the story, here it is. On December 11, I got sick. I had severe abdominal pain, a fever, chills, and generally felt like I had the flu. I just figured it was some kind of flu, so I did the usual: bed, fluids, Advil, etc. I actually even worked during most of it. By the weekend the fever and chills were gone, but the abdominal pain persisted. Because much of it was in the lower right quadrant I was a little concerned about an appendicitis. We were coming up on the Christmas holiday long weekend, and Gary, Toby and I were leaving for skiing and snow shoeing in Yosemite on December 27.

So I somewhat sheepishly called my wonderful primary care doc and he saw me the Thursday before Christmas. I was in pretty good shape by then and I thought he would say, "Go away, there's nothing wrong with you." To my surprise he said it could be a "smoldering appendicitis" and he didn't want to take any chances with a long holiday weekend ahead. So he sent me to the hospital for a lower abdominal CT scan.

He called back the same night to say my appendix was fine, but the scan showed, "Something I didn't expect," all of these swollen retroperitoneal lymph nodes. He had me do some blood work, sent me off to Yosemite with his blessing and left a message that I received when I returned saying my blood work was "normal, normal, normal."

We all felt, how could there be anything seriously wrong? But he wanted to do an upper abdominal and thorax CT scan to see if there were swollen nodes higher up. The scan came back showing all the previous nodes much more enlarged and many more higher up: a bad sign. I then went in for a needle biopsy of one of the abdominal nodes and the pathology report showed cancer cells. A further analysis diagnosed non-Hodgkins lymphoma.

I've had one more bout of the same pain, chills, and fever just last week, which my oncologist tells me is the lymphoma. Thank God for my wonderful doctor and that first CT scan or I'm sure I'd be oblivious.

Message to all of you: if anything at all unusual happens in your body, check it out!!!

As you can imagine, I'm scared out of my mind and at the same time I can't believe this is actually happening to me. It comes so completely out of the blue. I keep thinking of our kids playing capture the flag where one of the best strategies is to create a disturbance up front so everyone is preoccupied, and then send the little guy in around the back to get the flag.

I've been out here warding off the car wreck, the clogged arteries, the colon cancer, the breast cancer, the heart attack, the stroke, and little guy lymphoma sneaks in the back and grabs the flag. Or maybe it's like the illusionist enchanting our eyes with the brightly colored silk cloth while he deftly produces the coin from his sleeve.

So the obvious question is, why did this happen, and the unequivocal answer is: no one knows. Apparently I had some vulnerable gene that met, maybe over the course of many years, with some kind of environmental assault.

Could it be that my beloved, idyllic, country childhood in South Dakota dosed me with Midwest crop pesticides that finally unleashed their destruction? Or maybe it was my wayward experimentation as a hippy (I was the flower child, nature girl variety) that tweaked a few chromosomes.

In our desperation to understand, my sister has thrown out the hypothesis that maybe it was drinking water from the old farm cistern where my musician boyfriend and I briefly lived on a commune. Then, of course moving forward in time, we have the vineyards - more pesticides, and plastic water bottles and cell phones and microwaves and automobile emissions, or maybe that childhood trip through the Arizona desert in the '50s, before anyone really thought about what did happen after all those nuclear tests. But obviously for each possibility there are hundreds of us exposed to the same thing who don't have lymphoma.

You all know me, I'll quickly move on to the metaphoric, mystical planes.

As I understand it, what happens with a lymphoma is that there is a transmutation on the genetic level and formerly functional cells first begin to grow larger and proliferate, and then they actually figure out how to become immortal. Because they don't die, things clog up; new young lymphocytes are trying to grow and take their place but the immortal ones don't make room. (Sounds a bit like complaints about us baby boomers!)

So, I'd say this is about letting go, what do you think? Yep, impermanence and letting go. Well, my first step is taking this leave from my work. I hope that opens up time and space to look at what else I need to let go of; nope, those lymphocytes just don't get to be immortal and neither does anything else on this plane of existence.

An odd premonition: I guess my intuition is intact. We celebrated Gary's 60th birthday January 7 and I caught myself thinking, "Now that we're moving into our 60s our friends will probably begin to have some health issues. I wonder who will be the first to have a cancer." Be careful what you think!

So thank you all for being out there for me. What a comfort to know you all care. If you cross paths with my son, Toby, in person or on the phone, I'm sure he would appreciate keeping life as normal as possible; more focus on his life, less on my being sick. I appreciate all prayers and good thoughts. I think I'm embarking on the challenge of my life. Gary is being the saint that he truly is, but I'm guessing he's going to need a lot of support.

Sorry to be the messenger of difficult news. I hope you are all healthy; that concept has taken on a whole new significance for me! Toby gave me a CD of some of his favorite music for Christmas and a line in one of the songs jumped out at me today, " ... and it came to me then, that every plan is a tiny prayer to father time..."

I intend to be making plans, and I hope you'll make some for me, too.

Much love,

Susan

19

Apoptosis and Impermanence: Entering the Land of Letting Go

At the same time I am writing this email, I am frantically trying to understand what is happening with my body. My oncologist is very patient and thorough, describing what he sees through a Western perspective: there is a disruption of a process in the normal life of a cell.

Every normal cell has a life span and at the end of its life a very complicated series of chemical reactions happens, which essentially causes the cell to die. This cell death is natural and is called apoptosis.

In the case of my cancer, there is a change in my actual genes that is causing the processes responsible for apoptosis in my malignant cells to be altered. This essentially allows these altered cells to become immortal: they have lost the ability to die. The problem is that the whole health of the system is predicated on a cycle: cells are born, grow, serve a purpose and then die, so new, young healthy cells can come into being, take their place in the system, do their work and eventually wear out and die as well. Ironically, it is the ability of the individual cells to let go and die that allows the organism to continue to live.

If the cells are not moving on, a tumor forms, and eventually the tumors negatively impact the functioning of organs and the healthy functioning of the whole system. My actual physical body is having trouble letting go, and that inability to let go is threatening to destroy the entire system.

Amazingly, at the same time I am learning about apoptosis, Yuan Miao, who does not yet know I have cancer, is focusing in our Blue Pearl meetings on the concept of impermanence. This is a central tenet of many Buddhist traditions, and I have meditated on it often over the years.

The idea is that everything is essentially impermanent. The Buddhist teaching is that suffering comes from either trying to grasp onto things, or from rejecting things as they are, because of not recognizing, or refusing to accept, the inevitability of impermanence. By accepting impermanence we can more fully embrace and value our life as it is at this moment.

Knowing that even the most wonderful things in our life are impermanent, we are motivated to stay present, and fully appreciate them while we can. When they naturally pass, we can more easily let them go and embrace what comes next.

Knowing that the unpleasant things in life are also impermanent, we can resist less and find what there is to learn from them, knowing that they, too, will pass. The challenge is to meet life as it is with no attachment, no aversion. An inability to embrace impermanence separates us from the pulse of life and the life force of the universe.

It is the nature of energy to keep moving: form arises, form dissolves, over and over in a beautiful, rhythmic dance. When we are one with that dance we are healthy and vibrant; when we are out of step we experience suffering in many ways: emotionally, physically, mentally and spiritually.

Facing my own mortality, I am suddenly insatiably interested in my ancestors. Realizing that an individual life really does pass by in the blink of an eye, I long to feel part of a longer continuum. But I am also inspired by an insistent, unrelenting voice in my head saying, "Keep searching. Your lineage holds the clue you are looking for." Like the siren's song it keeps me up at night.

My lineage. I too have a lineage. Attending the Blue Pearl meetings, I have been fascinated with learning the teachings and practices of Yuan Miao's Eastern lineage, transmitted to her by her grandmother. But as I search for truths and teachings that might help me as I confront a life-threatening condition, I realize that I also have a Western lineage passed down to me through my own ancestors. Suddenly a detective, I pour over the unpublished family history manuscripts, lovingly written by my mother toward the end of her life when she was facing her own mortality.

And then one night at just past 2:00 A.M. a word I had heard and read many times as I investigated my family history jumps out at me: the *Reformation*. Re-formation. I am running to our room and shaking Gary awake. "The Reformation! Re-formation! Form dissolving into formlessness and reforming. Impermanence. My lineage comes directly from people who learned to let go."

With the patience he always had when our son was up in the night as a baby, he sits up, turns on the light and says, "What exactly are you talking about?"

"The Reformation. My mom traced our family history back as far as the 1500s in Europe and the Reformation."

"And why all the excitement about that now?"

"Gary, everything I'm learning about the cancer is that I have to let go. What does it mean to let go? Old forms have to dissolve, like the old cells, so new forms can arise. Miao has been stressing impermanence. My personal lineage comes directly from Germans who rebelled against the most entrenched form of their time: the Roman Catholic Church and all the powerful economic and political forces associated with it. But they managed to go through a re-formation."

I have followed him to the kitchen where he is now slicing up an avocado for a sandwich. He hands me a glass of milk. "You may be on to something. I seem to remember that Martin Luther—wasn't he a German priest?—originally only envisioned reforming abuses within the

Catholic Church, but eventually it became clear that it would be necessary to challenge the authority of the Church itself. Remember? People were questioning the relationship between man and god, and therefore also between man and the Pope, who was believed to be directly appointed by God. I think there was a lot of disillusion with the office of the Pope anyway because of accusations of corruption. It wasn't going to be enough to just revise the existing form. The whole thing was going to have to collapse and be reformed."

A look passes between us. Exactly what form might have to collapse for me?

I take a bite of my sandwich. "Well, what I'm learning from my ancestors is that changing form and transformation don't necessarily happen easily. Listen to what my mom's book says about my dad's side of our family: 'Michael Sattler, who was probably one of Ted's early ancestors, was directly influenced by Martin Luther. He had been a prior of a Benedictine monastery in Germany, but because of the influence of Martin Luther's ideas he decided to forsake the monastery and to marry.'"

"Hmmm, that can't have ended well." He's fondly brushing my hair out of my eyes.

"Well, apparently he was extremely revolutionary and he became quite prominent in the Anabaptist Movement. One of their radical ideas was that they questioned infant baptisms as a way to ensure salvation. They promoted the idea of adult baptism, believing people needed to ***choose*** to be baptized. One night, in Switzerland, the Anabaptists met by the river and performed adult baptisms on each other! Back then this was truly a revolutionary act: a VERY big deal. Eventually the guy who was their leader was arrested for doing it, tried and sentenced to execution by being *drowned* in the Limmat River!"

"Anyway, it says in my mom's book that Michael fled back to Strasburg – that's where my ancestors are officially documented, beginning in 1550—where he promoted the idea of separation of church and state;

he wanted a totally self-governing church, free of government interference, with decisions made by the whole congregation, and he advocated doing away with tithes, usury, and military service. He apparently promoted pacifism, but he was eventually arrested and imprisoned on a whole host of counts: forsaking the order, marrying, refusing the making of oaths to the government, advocating refusal to wage war, and, get this, despising the mother of God! I think that had to do with his belief that Mary could not act as an intercessor with God. In general I think followers of Martin Luther believed we could have our own, direct relationship with god—that we didn't need *any* intercessor. And, no it definitely did not end well. After a two-day trial, his tongue was cut out, his flesh was torn six times with red-hot tongs and he was burned at the stake."

Gary's eyebrows have gone up. "Serious push-back."

"Well, my understanding is that because the Roman Catholic Church controlled everything at the time, the Reformation inevitably included political and economic issues. There was a belief that religious uniformity was necessary for political and social stability, so challenging the Roman Catholic Church could be considered treason. Consequently, people were arrested and tried for their beliefs, and some, like Michael Sattler, met with amazingly harsh punishments."

We make our way back to bed where Gary is soon relaxed and snoring, apparently not bothered by the red hot tongs.

I am wide- awake, remembering the story my mother told me about visiting the protestant church, Evang, Stadkirche, in Beitigheim, Germany with my dad, where she had tracked down our ancestors. The pastor there showed them an old leather book with entry after entry for Sattlers—my dad's forbearers—beginning with Kaspar Sattler, 1550, from whom he is directly descended. They were holding a church registry with 440-year-old original entries, naming some of the first people to break away from the Roman Catholic Church to form something brand new, and many of them share my DNA.

I'm thinking how fascinating it is that my mother replicated their revolutionary act, leaving the catholic church in which she—coming from a proper Irish/Catholic family– was raised, to marry my dad, a protestant, descended from these first participants in the Reformation.

If I had really been thinking about my ancestors the night of Miao's workshop when I began my journey into the realms of transformation, I would have realized that old forms do not give up easily, and that while the phoenix can indeed rise from the ashes, there is often a serious fire to be endured first.

It's a staggering thought that the Reformation caused Europe to be torn by civil and foreign wars for almost 150 years. It took that long for change of form to take place. Eventually evolution prevailed, and the old form had to dissolve so true re-formation, true transformation could occur.

I slide under the covers and conform to Gary's warm body. Feeling the reassuring rise and fall of his breath, I drift off to sleep, marveling that deep in my family DNA lies the experience of finding the courage, faith and trust to surrender the old form and tolerate the resulting formlessness which inevitably precedes re-formation. Not only were my ancestors pioneers, but they also form a long lineage of people who questioned the status quo.

The last thing I remember before falling asleep is a beautiful image of ancient, holy people dancing together in a place that is neither China and Tibet nor Europe, but somehow both. They weave in and out creating beautiful and ever-changing patterns. I understand that this dance is a celebration of the beauty of impermanence.

PRACTICE

Embracing Impermanence

Day 1

Watch the clouds for at least five minutes. Notice how change is continuous. One form flows into another in an endless, fluid dance.

Day 2

Spend 10 minutes outside in nature. Take a deep breath, clear your mind and pay attention to the current season. Notice the state of the foliage. Is it moist and green, dry and brittle, flowering or going to seed? Sense the temperature. Notice the activity of the animals. Try to sense how this season has flowed gradually out of the last season, and how it is slowly transforming into the next.

Day 3

Without judgment, notice your reactions to things in your life that change or end. You could write about this in a journal. If you are having trouble seeing your reactions clearly, try this exercise. Select an object that is important to you in some way - something you particularly like or value (you don't need to overdo this - not necessary to select your wedding ring or new car), and either give it away or throw it away. Notice your thought process and emotions as you try to select something, and especially as you actually part with it.

Day 4

Create an intention to help you develop an accepting relationship with impermanence. In fact, impermanence is the reality, not the exception. Miao says that Westerners often act surprised, sad or angry when things change or end, but really impermanence is the natural order of things. Remember to make the intention positive and in present tense. An example I use is, "I honor what has been as I open to what is now."

Day 5

Choose a small change you are aware of within yourself and try to embrace it. For example, I notice I have to walk parts of trails where I used to be able to run for exercise. My knees can not take as much pounding as they once could. I try to focus on how much more I notice in my surroundings when I am walking, and how much more likely I am to see wildlife since my approach is quieter and calmer.

Day 6

Choose a small change you are aware of in a family member, loved one or friend and try to embrace it. I notice Toby's growing desire to spend more time with his friends and less time with me. I try to focus on how this allows me to reinvest time and energy in my relationship with Gary, and in my own life interests.

Day 7

Choose a change you are aware of in our society and try to embrace it. For example, in many households both partners have to work outside the home in order to meet monthly expenses. I try to focus on how this can help create a greater sense of equality in the relationship, and enhance both partners' self esteem.

20

Fathers, Sons and Grandfathers

Perhaps it was strands of this family DNA that supported subsequent generations of my ancestors as they emigrated first from Germany to Russia, because of the promise of free land and exemption from military conscription, and then to the United States. Having barely reached the tender age of 19, Johann Jakob Sattler, my paternal grandfather, a German born in Odessa, Russia, stoically said his goodbyes to his tearful mother, father and eight brothers and sisters who were staying behind in Russia, and emigrated alone to the United States in 1877. His goal was to find a woman he knew only as Barbara Beck, his mother's sister who was living in a small South Dakota town.

He journeyed alone across a turbulent Atlantic Ocean and half a fledgling American continent, until he found his pioneering aunt on the frontier prairie, and began a new life in a new world. He arrived in a country in transition; impermanence was the order of the day. Old forms were rapidly dissolving, constant reminders that nothing lasts forever. Bands of Lakota Sioux Native Americans still roamed across what had always been their land, setting up their teepee villages and charging across the plains on horseback after herds of magnificent black bison, looking like huge dark storms rolling over the prairie. The Sioux Nation was still strong, but gold had been discovered in the Black Hills, prospectors wanted access to the area and the United States Government had dispatched General George Custer to effect a treaty and move the Lakota onto reservation lands. This precipitated the Lakota war of 1876-1877, including the famous Battle of the Little Big Horn in which Custer was defeated, fought the year before my grandfather arrived.

The Sioux were a deeply spiritual people. The South Dakota land vibrated with their drumming, dancing feet at pow-wows, chanting, and fervent prayers to the Great Spirit. My grandfather's decision to settle on this land at this point in history, created the conditions that would make it possible for me to learn wisdom from a Native American spiritual lineage. It would be on this sacred ground that I would eventually receive teachings from the Sioux Medicine Man.

It was also on this land that my grandfather would have a powerful spiritual experience that would change *his* life, directly connecting him to the Christian lineage of his ancestors. He would pass that lineage on to my father, and my father and mother in turn would pass it on to me.

Young, curious and wanting to experience more of what life had to offer, Johann Jakob tired of helping his aunt and uncle farm. One morning he focused his hazel eyes in a steady gaze at the horizon, saddled up his fiery black stallion, and rode out across the plains. Eventually, he came across a country revival meeting of the kind that were flourishing in the United States in the late 1800s. Entering one of the off-white canvas tents commonly set up in a farmer's pasture, its flaps beating a steady rhythm to the prairie winds, he must have been excited by the crowds of new people, some of whom had traveled long distances in buggies and on horseback to witness the healings and conversions they had heard about. I'm sure it must have been a charismatic young preacher, full of fire and brimstone, his face lit up with religious zeal, who strode across the stage, imploring those who needed to be healed to come forward.

According to the folks in attendance, amazing healings occurred as the preacher "laid on hands" during that revival. My grandfather notes in his personal papers that on that day he was "awakened to the spirit." I wonder what that meant for him. Something powerful obviously happened to him that day, and I don't think it was only about understanding new religious concepts. He had an *experience.* Perhaps my grandfather experienced the vibration of a higher level of spiritual consciousness, causing him to feel "awakened."

A few days later, a white envelope slipped from his hand, the discarded shell of tragic news from his homeland. "We're sorry to inform you that your father was found frozen to death in a terrible blizzard. We are so sorry."

I wonder if time stood still for my grandfather when he received the news, like it did for me when I received the news about my client's death. End of life, the end of innocence for a son. Perhaps this was his own first tragedy calling him to transformation.

Already fueled with the passion of the revival meeting, he decided to make his life's work ministering to the spirit. Carrying on the lineage from his ancestors, going back to at least the Reformation, he became an ordained minister in 1888 and served as the pastor of a Congregational Church in Chicago for seven years. But to me, his most important work came following a decision he made after holding the hand of his fragile, young wife of four years and watching her suffer with typhoid fever.

"Hold on, Anna. Please hold on. I still need you."

As his unanswered prayer echoed away, her death became a second trauma, after the early loss of his father, calling on him to wrestle with the reality that "we can't control everything that happens."

Deciding to leave Chicago, Johann Jakob returned to the frontiers of South Dakota, Nebraska and Colorado, where he worked as a circuit rider. On any particular Sunday, he harnessed his beloved steel gray gelding to his old black buggy, and traveled to fledgling communities too new and too small to have a church. Preaching, organizing and generally ministering to German immigrants trying to endure settlement hardships, he tried to help them bear the separation from their homeland.

By now his own first-hand experiences with the loss of father and wife had taught him valuable lessons about how life calls on us to learn to let go and surrender, and about the timeless, spiritual realm that remains when everything else falls away. Together those early pioneers of the plains must have grappled with issues of trust, struggled to remain courageous, and looked to my grandfather to help them nourish the light of faith.

What a strange coincidence that this was just three years after the brutal Battle at Wounded Knee, which insured that the Lakota would lose *their* homeland. As they were severed from their sacred land, the Black Hills, their Paha Sapa, and forced onto reservations, they felt severed from their spirituality. They too must have struggled to maintain courage and trust and looked to their leaders for inspiration. Two peoples who had waged a bitter war over land were left to confront similar internal struggles. As my grandfather was reminding European settlers cut off from their homeland, "You have to have faith," I'm sure there were powerful Lakota medicine men offering their people the mantra, "Don't stop. Keep going."

I wish I had known my grandfather, that I could have talked with him about his spiritual journey and heard his words of wisdom. But after thirty-seven years of ministering, when his son, my father, was only eleven years old, my grandfather felt sudden crushing pain in his chest one day as he walked near his home.

Clutching his chest and struggling to catch his breath, he collapsed on the street. My grandfather was dead, leaving a child of another generation to grapple with his own crisis of meaning when he wasn't able to control life events. This child, my father, who was named Theodore Herbert, was the youngest of six children.

My grandfather was survived by his second wife, Paulina, a petite, dark-eyed, dark-haired beauty. With six children to raise, she never worked outside the home, and when her husband, my grandfather, collapsed with that fatal heart attack, she was left with only the generosity of the church and the efforts of the oldest siblings to help take care of her and her children.

Only eleven years old, my father, then called Teddy, had to dig deep to find courage and trust after the death of his father. With that look of startled bewilderment worn by children experiencing sudden trauma, and a cotton newspaper bag slung over his shoulder, he walked the length of train cars making a stop at the local depot. I'm sure that again and again his hand went to his pocket, checking to see that his money was still there, because even the few coins earned from those buying the daily paper helped his family survive.

His father had answered the challenge of surrender to loss by ministering to the spirit, helping people stay connected to what he believed was everlasting. Together in church they repeated the words of the doxology, a mantra energized by group repetition over several hundred years, "Glory be to the Father, to the Son, and to the Holy Spirit. As it was in the beginning is now and ever shall be, world without end." And, connecting with the primordial, healing sound of Aaaa, they added, "Amen."

I wonder exactly when it was that my father responded to our inability to control everything that happens and made his decision to become a medical doctor, committing his life to extending love and compassion in an effort to alleviate suffering.

I think of my grandfather at age 19, receiving the letter telling him of his father's death in the Russian blizzard. I think of my father receiving the news at age eleven of his father's heart attack. And now one of the first steps in my own process of letting go is to disclose the cancer diagnosis to my 16-year-old son, Toby.

A son of another generation will embark on *his* quest to meet the reality that, you can't control everything that happens. I grieve his loss of innocence, his childhood cocoon of utter security and safety. I try to believe that we can all weather the impending change of form in our family, our own personal Reformation.

As we burrow into the cozy green leather couches in our family room where over the years we have watched everything from *Winnie the Pooh* movies to *Pulp Fiction*, we try to be honest, but hopeful; real, but not dramatic. With his bright, blue eyes peering out from under his protective shock of long blond hair, he meets the news with concern, but not surprise, having watched me traipsing off to increasing numbers of medical appointments over the past month.

He asks several questions about the course of treatment, and then with the bluntness of a teenager, he articulates one of my greatest fears.

"Are we going to be poor?"

When I dropped those letters to my clients through the mail slot, huddling under my relief and even elation was this same fearful question, and I don't know the answer yet.

I am trying to trust a power greater than myself to help this process along, if I can only move out of the way. But will we be poor? As I sit, wanting to reassure both myself and my sensitive son, I sense the spiritual complexity which, for me, is embedded in that question. The complicated answer will have to continue to evolve over a very long time. For now, I am immersed in trying to let go of the fear associated with that thought so I can courageously step into unknown territory.

My grandfather and his wife.

Reverend Sattler.

21

Shining Spirits Surround Me

From: **Susan Sattler**
Date: **Feb. 7, 2007 9:05 PM**
Subject: **Susan sends her love and updates**

To all of my friends,

You are such a beautiful, shining group of spirits! Thank you for your immediate, heartfelt outpouring of love, support, offers for help of all kinds and even humor at such a difficult time. I am 100% sure that it is the gift of all this love and radiant energy beamed my way that is going to heal me; I know it's already begun.

This week I have formally taken an indefinite leave from my psychotherapy practice of twenty-three years. Sadly it had to be abrupt, and I had to spend time lining up therapists to take over the care of my clients and facilitating that transition with as much care and sensitivity as possible.

I also have been in the midst of an incredible number of medical appointments with a whole team of doctors. We're still in the diagnostic stage: as I told you, no question that this is a malignant lymphoma, but there are all different varieties and mine does not seem to fit the standard classifications. Mine comes up on pathology more like a follicular lymphoma, but behaves clinically more like a diffuse one. But get this, they actually can transform over time, so they think mine might be in the process of transforming before our very eyes.

So, they are sending me to get a second opinion at Stanford Hospital (which apparently is the state of the art place to go if you have lymphoma), hoping their team of giant-brained people will be able to pinpoint this. I may also qualify for a clinical trial. My oncologist there has a magnificent name: Ranjana. I think it's beautiful, and when this is over I plan to steal her identity. No seriously, if it turns out that she is a Hindu I may just ask for a good word with her spiritual master. (Of course we'll be only talking scientifically, so I'll probably never know.) My sister says she is probably a Sikh, are they not also Hindu? I need to bone up on my Indian religious traditions.

Anyway, the appointment is on Valentine's Day; I take that as a positive sign. After that appointment, the Stanford team reviews my case, consults with my local oncologist and they decide on the final treatment protocol. Then we begin treatment as fast as possible.

So, the general update is that it is now unlikely I'll actually be doing chemo before the middle of the week after Valentine's Day, and guess what, my birthday is February 22, so there is a very good possibility I could begin chemo that day! I see it as an excellent metaphor—a new birth—my birth day—the day my new life begins (without this lymphoma getting in the way).

In the meantime, so far, we are doing OK. We have our ups and downs emotionally, but we're trying to maintain a sense of humor and in many ways this is a very tender, loving time.

Again, thank you for all the offers of help. I think our greatest needs will be when I begin actual treatment, but we'll see. Some days the pain, fevers and general exhaustion that are part of the lymphoma are fairly debilitating, other days I feel pretty good. My wonderful, saintly neighbor, Sheila, has offered to be my point person in terms of coordinating help. If you'd like to be on her list to help, you could let her know.

With deep gratitude and love,

Susan

22

Guan Shi Yin Pu Sa and Heart Connections

Guan Shi Yin Pu Sa,
Guan Shi Yin Pu Sa.
Da Tz Da Bei,
Guang Da Ling Gan,
Guan Shi Yin Pu Sa

Ya, La Suo,
Guan Shi Yin Pu Sa,
Ta Shi Te Lek,
Guan Shi Yin Pu Sa

Miao is dressed in green silk, bending over her Chinese harp and singing as we begin our bi-monthly Blue Pearl Group. Next to her on a makeshift altar is a carved wooden statue of Guan Yin, standing, looking down, her long robe swirling gracefully around her. She holds an inverted vase in one hand.

"Guan Shi Yin is the one who hears the cries of the world," Miao states firmly as she holds us in her timeless presence. "Yes, she hears your cries. I know this. *Da tz, Da bei*, great wisdom, great compassion. *Guang da ling gan*, great magical power." We absorb this as we linger in the now familiar space between thoughts.

"She is the bodhisattva of compassion, mercy and unconditional love. You may know her as an elegant Chinese lady, but she takes many forms. She is not bound by religious tradition. When we cry out to Guan Shi Yin Pu Sa, we might be reaching to Mother Mary, or Mohammad, or Jesus, our great grandmother, our ancestors, or any beings we feel are our guides and protectors. Yes, this is very powerful. The Blue Pearl represents the precious jewel of our inner nature, within which is the wisdom and compassion of Guan Yin."

You could easily hear a pin drop for several minutes as we connect with Miao's perfect presence: no past, no future, no thoughts, only pure awareness infused with the love, compassion and mercy of Guan Yin.

As my thinking mind slowly reboots, I realize that I experienced the power of this compassion, mercy and love the first night I met Miao and heard her mantric singing. As I grieved the death of my client, I believe Guan Shi Yin Pu Sa heard my cries and helped me meet Miao so her mantric singing could transform my grief and trauma. Do I understand how this could really happen? No. This is obviously the point where we either insist on and cling to rationality, or take some kind of a leap into faith and mysticism.

When my mother died a year later, I received a second gift, the opportunity to continue to deepen my connection with Guan Yin and Yuan Miao through the Blue Pearl meetings. Bereft of my mother, I soaked up the mothering energy of Yuan Miao. I don't think it is any coincidence that the spiritual teacher who appeared in my life at that time was a woman.

Miao emphasizes that Guan Yin represents a collection of entities. She says that when we cry out to her we might be crying out to "any beings we feel are our guides," but for me it is significant that she is represented in female form. Through my participation in the Blue Pearl groups, and my conscious nurturing of a relationship with Guan Yin, I begin to experience that through her I can connect with the universal mother, the creative source in the universe. That feels like an everlasting source. My mother died, Miao is in physical form—she will have a physical death one day too—but I sense that the universal mother is eternal.

When I received the cancer diagnosis, I once again sent my cries for love and compassion and healing to Guan Yin. In my private moments I would cry out, "I just want my mother." I wanted that sense of safety and security, nurturing and comfort that she provided when I was a child. It seemed like some kind of cruel cosmic joke that the first time in my life that I had an illness serious enough to actually threaten my life, was right after my mother's death when she wouldn't be there to support and comfort me—at least not in physical form.

But Guan Yin is a bodhisattva who embodies the compassion of all the Buddhas, and is sometimes represented with a thousand hands available to aid in helping the suffering multitudes. When I cried out to Guan Yin after my diagnosis of cancer, she mobilized her many loving, helping hands.

An immediate answer to my cries came through my friends. The response to my email letting people know about my diagnosis was truly astounding. From day one, there was an amazing outpouring of love. I had a continuous image of my friends and family, their hearts open, with golden light literally pouring out towards me. Here are some examples of the many emails I received in those first days:

Titled *Showering you with light*, "I want to put my arms around you and give you healing, loving light."

"We will rally the troops and you are not alone—we love you—what do you need right now—we are here."

"If you'd like, I will immediately put you on our prayer tree and ask everyone to send you good wishes. Whatever I can do in any personal way, please let me know. I'll be holding you in my heart daily."

"I can help you by cooking or driving you or whatever you may need. Or even call you and tell you jokes (although I only know two), just know I am holding you in my heart."

"All of us out here want you to know that we are here for you in every way, creating webs of emotional and psychic support, sending healing energy and prayers, and at any moment just being there to hold your hand."

And from my sister, Ann, who has been my most loyal protector all of my life, "You are the same little sister who used to jump up and hop right back on when Molly (my horse) tried to roll you off on the ground, or Dude bucked you off, or you fell off your bike on the wet pavement and cut your forehead and got right back up.... or did a triple flip off the high diving board at age 5.... visualize yourself as that kid. We all love you."

It honestly seemed to me that a huge crack had opened up in the universe and love and light were pouring through everyone I knew. A woman whom I had met only briefly one time at a luncheon several months before called to say she was bringing a hot dinner to me. A woman I had not seen in at least two years who knew me when I was the team mom for Toby's soccer team, appeared at my door with a large pile of CDs with sound healing, healing visualizations, healing music and a DVD with a wonderful little Chinese man leading Qigong.

So, it came as no surprise to me that my first appointment with the Stanford oncologist was scheduled for Valentine's Day. It was only one more event in a long string of "coincidences" that began the evening that Miao "happened" to appear just when I needed her. I was to begin my journey through the land of Western medicine treatment options on a day reserved for the entire country to be focused on love.

Guan Yin "hears the cries of the world."

23

Valentines and Clinical Trials

From: **Susan Sattler**
Date: **Feb. 16, 2007 4:42 PM**
Subject: **Update on Susan Sattler's Journey**

Hi to all,

So, I'd much rather be reporting in on the great trek we had today through the Himalayas in Nepal, but I guess that has to wait for now. In fact, the trek Gary and I made was through the Marin County rush hour traffic, across the ever-spectacular Golden Gate Bridge, out 19th Avenue and down the peninsula to my old stomping grounds at Stanford.

I can't begin to tell you how surreal it was to be looking for the signs for Cancer Center and to be walking into this huge (and actually quite beautiful) building called Stanford Advanced Medicine Center. I kept having this feeling that somehow I had stumbled through some kind of weird science fiction wormhole into a parallel universe where I was now living someone else's life, some other

Susan Sattler, who has much worse luck and is much less healthy than I; or that I had stumbled onto the wrong movie set and I was now in the wrong movie, not my movie at all. But, alas, I keep waking up each morning and rediscovering that this is all actually happening to me.

So here's the scoop. After waiting for two hours, I was finally seen by one of the fellows, someone who has finished medical school, post graduate training, and is doing a year of specialized training. She looked to me to be at most sixteen years old, she could have easily passed on any high school campus. Does it seem that the entire world is now being run by children? This Susan Sattler in the parallel universe has to realize she's not the young thing anymore.

Then after another hour wait I finally got to meet Ranjana, the doctor with the beautiful name. I liked her in a completely different way than I expected: definitely not the warm, fuzzy nurturer, but obviously very smart and willing to explain things in depth, but at a speed that made all my synapses fire away at break-neck speed.

So, we've got the diagnosis down, I have a follicular large B-cell diffuse (3B) lymphoma, Stage 3 (meaning it is dispersed both above and below the diaphragm, but not spread to other organ systems), Grade 3 (which means it is considered aggressive in its progression).

This all means it probably is in the process of transforming from a more defined structure (follicular) to a less defined structure (diffuse), not a good sign. So, it's critical to begin treatment right away, and I'm assuming the doctor will outline the specific treatment I have to do. But no, none of this can be that easy. She says the standard of care for a long time now is what they call R-CHOP chemotherapy.

I can do that, or she offers me the option of being in a clinical trial at Stanford where I will be randomly assigned to one of two arms of a study, one of which is the R-CHOP and the other is the CHOP followed by a newer drug, Bexxar, which has shown promise for helping people achieve longer what they call "disease-free survival" (isn't that an interesting term).

So, the clinical studies' nurse then comes in and completely terrifies me by making sure I've been fully informed of all the risks and possible adverse side effects of both arms of treatment and tells me to think about it and get back to her. Gary and I stumble out of there at 6:30 P.M. (we're the last patients in the building), completely overwhelmed.

Unfortunately, I was catapulted into my first real breakdown; it all just seemed too much. Even with all my obsessive researching online I'm not an oncologist and the depth of understanding I felt I needed to make the decision seemed beyond me. I sent off a list of questions to the doctor with the beautiful name who amazingly called me right back. She carefully responded to my questions, but finally said, curtly, "You're asking questions which won't be answered for ten to fifteen years. You should have been a scientist."

So, I have to make decisions that may affect whether, or how long, I may live based on questions that have no answers! I spoke directly with my local oncologist (who talked with me for forty-five minutes), and he finally said firmly, "You should do the clinical trial." He felt the Bexxar arm had the potential to significantly increase the time of disease free survival.

So, I got on the phone and signed up for the study. It was a relief to feel I'm moving on. No guarantee which arm I'll be in, but either way I have to do the treatment at Stanford.

Now we have to do the insurance shuffle, set up last scans and blood work and tests, and then, as I predicted, there's a chance I'll begin treatment Feb. 22, my birthday.

Again, I want to thank all of you for your wonderful outpouring of love, emails, food, cards and flowers. I've been in a lot more pain. It's amazing how difficult pain makes it to function. I'm trying to take a deep breath and go into this as one more life experience that will help me grow in all ways.

Love and gratitude,

Susan

24

Medicine Wheels and Finger Yoga

The busyness of my psychotherapy practice and usual daily life fell away weeks ago with the initial diagnosis of cancer. But I realize that I have quickly replaced it with an array of appointments for doctor consultations, scans of all parts of my body, phone conversations with family and friends, and hours of obsessive research on the computer about lymphoma.

It is only now, as final medical decisions have been made and a course of Western treatment is in place that a space opens up for me to reconnect with my inner being. I fully intend to take advantage of all that Western medicine has to offer me, but what about my own wisdom? How am I actually going to be active in my healing process? How will I spend my days now that there is an open space? What about my revelation that my "treatment" could be a blend of many traditions, representing many parts that make up the whole of me?

As I lie on my living room floor, an image of the Lakota medicine wheel floats behind my closed eyes. The first one I saw was at the Indian Studies Center where I worked in South Dakota. It was a hoop that hung above the doorway. There was a cross in the center and the circle of the hoop connected the four ends of the cross. Each of the four sections of the hoop created by the cross were wrapped in material of four different colors: yellow, red, black, and white. There were seven white feathers at the bottom, hanging from leather strips decorated with beads.

When I asked my student, Jessie, to tell me about it, there was an awkward silence. Looking up at me through her black bangs, she said, "I'm sorry, Miss Sattler, only the medicine man can give you that medicine, but I can try to arrange for you to see him."

Two days later, I traveled onto the reservation with Jessie and sat on the steps of a tiny house with the elderly man who was holding a medicine wheel. Enjoying the spring sunlight, I closed my eyes and listened carefully as he passed on his ancient wisdom. "The circle represents the togetherness of all things; everything is connected, on and off the earth. *Mitakuye Oyasin*, all my relations. We are part of infinitely connecting circles of life, our families, our villages, our countries, the universe. Everything comes back around again. Everything is connected. The cross there forms four points that might seem to be opposite, but they are still connected, represented by the circle. The points of the cross first of all represent the four directions, north, south, east, and west. There are also the fifth and sixth directions of up (the sky) and down (the earth) and a seventh direction that is within. The points of the cross also represent many other things, like the gifts of the four directions: air from the north, water from the south, fire from the east, and earth from the west—all connected by the circle."

He pauses. I open my eyes to assure him I'm fully engaged. He squints at me as if sizing me up. I was young, only 22 years old at the time, but even then I was a spiritual seeker.

Perhaps he sensed that, because he continued, "The wheel also teaches us about what a person is. The four ends of the cross represent mental in the north (our mind), spiritual in the east (our soul), emotional in the south (our heart), and physical in the west (our body). The person is at the center of the wheel and is in charge of all the other aspects. Little girl, you *are* the direction of within. The inner part of each of us moves beyond time and beyond seasons. This direction is where we unite with the Great Mystery. *You* must take care of your mind, your soul, your heart and your body. Then you can be one with the Great Spirit. Illness happens when there is an imbalance in the wheel. The medicine man can help people get back in balance. He might use prayer or chanting, give you some herbs, but you need to help with your own healing when your wheel is out of balance."

Young and healthy at the time, I was not sure why he was emphasizing this, but I now wonder if he had slipped into some clairvoyant state, knowing the day would come when I would need these words of wisdom.

I'm wondering how my wheel has become so out of balance that it may have contributed to the manifestation of cancer. I vow to reconnect to the teaching of the Lakota medicine man. It is time for me to nurture equally my mind, my soul, my heart and my body. I will look to all my teachers and healers, East/West, modern/ancient, male/female for guidance, but I am at the center of my circle and I intend to be active in my own healing.

Lying on the floor beside me is Miao's DVD that I spontaneously purchased at our last Blue Pearl Group. Simply looking at the cover that night transported me into that timeless, open, peaceful place I had come to connect with being in her presence. Now, looking more carefully at the photograph on the DVD cover, I realize Miao is forming a mudra, right hand creating a shape at her heart, and left holding another shape below, closer to her abdomen. I immediately feel a sense of calm and gratitude. What am I grateful for? It is just a spontaneous feeling, similar to love. Looking at the cover of the DVD I feel grateful for life, for the universe, for all that is. Mantras from my other lineages echo in my mind, "Praise God from whom all blessings flow...." "*Wakan Tanka Tunkasila, Pilamaye Ye.*" (Great Spirit, great grandfather, I thank you.)

I see now that this is a teaching DVD. In the first part, Miao demonstrates eleven mudras that are to be practiced along with mantric vibrational chanting and visualization of specific colors. She says they are especially designed to address today's health issues.

"Well," I'm thinking, "I seem to have manifested one of the most common health issues in the Western world today. Perhaps these mudras and mantras can help me transform it." When I look at the one on the cover, it certainly affects me in a much more positive way than when my well-intentioned friend demonstrated how I could just flip cancer the bird, causing me to flinch instinctively.

Pulling out my meditation cushion and my laptop, I put on the DVD and begin following along. I have an implicit trust in Miao. I believe that she is an evolved being; the truth is, I believe she is enlightened. She created this DVD because she thought it could help alleviate suffering, so I am willing to commit myself to it wholeheartedly.

Some of the mudras on the DVD are relatively easy to follow; some are unbelievably complex. Taking full advantage of living in the modern technological age, I use the reverse arrow shamelessly, scrutinizing what she is doing with her hands.

The very first mudra is for balancing the endocrine system. Forming two circles by touching nails of index fingers to tips of thumbs, I touch these two circles so they look like eyeglasses in front of me. Then I extend middle and ring fingers and touch tips of right to tips of left. Spreading the little fingers as far away as possible, I touch their tips, stretch the whole configuration, turn it upside down and place it in front of my heart. This really is like doing yoga—it feels good at first (who hasn't ever put the tips of your fingers together, pressing and stretching both palms and fingers?), and then I reach my "edge," fingers shaking, and I have to back off to find "right effort," working hard enough, but not too hard. Miao's voice on the DVD is chanting, "Damo, Da, Hum Hum, Damo, Da Hum Hum, Damo Da Hum Hum." She suggests three specific colors to visualize as you do each mudra/mantra combination, so I am trying to remember to visualize grass green, light blue and deep purple.

A beginner, I find it is too much to try to remember the mantras myself, so I just listen to Miao's beautiful voice, letting the sounds wash over me. I try valiantly to remember to visualize the three colors that go with each mudra, but I find that within seconds I have forgotten them. The whole session becomes an exercise in managing my self-judgment, but through it all, I arrive at a peaceful place at the end, actually feeling refreshed and centered.

Spontaneously, I make a vow to do these mudras and mantras every day of my treatment. The vow comes out of simple faith; I trust Miao and I trust that there is an essential healing force in the universe. She is offering these mudras, mantras and color visualizations as one way to access this healing source.

25

Birthday Chemo: 'That's Good!"

From: **Susan Sattler**
Date: **Feb. 23, 2007 9:01 PM**
Subject: **Susan Sattler's Journey**

Hi Everyone,

So, here's the update.

Last Tuesday my oh-so-generous friend Jennifer came to my door and fetched me at 6:45 A.M. I was facing the day with the dreaded bone marrow aspiration, so she was a godsend, spending the day with me at the Stanford Cancer Center as I traipsed from blood draw to CT scan to bone marrow aspiration.

I had whined significantly enough about the last experience with the bone marrow aspiration that they agreed to give me a drug "lollipop" for pain before they did it. I love the euphemisms. I've had a pain "lollipop", and I will soon have a chemotherapy "cocktail". Anyway, either the lollipop worked or being at Stanford is paying off in terms of technique, because the aspiration was at least 100 times less painful than the original one.

After they had done all their final testing and probing, they were able to enter me into the clinical trial. I was randomized into the standard-of-care arm of the study. That, unfortunately means I do not get the new wonder drug, Bexxar. I would be lying if I said I wasn't disappointed, but I am so trying to grow through this experience.

I wrote early on that I think some of the lesson here is letting go, so I am letting go of the notion that the Bexxar would have been best for me and trying to really trust the universe that this path is the one I need to be on.

Some of you know that over the past three years I've been a follower of a wonderful Tibetan/ Chinese spiritual teacher. Her name is Yuan Miao and her grandmother was a spiritual master of a long Tibetan lineage. I truly love her in the deepest sense of the word. She has given all of us who study with her a kind of mantra: it is an immediate response to have to whatever happens, "That's good!!!!"

The idea is that we may not be able to understand the potential positive in all of life's happenings (especially if they seem sad or bad to us at the time), but we must have faith that in some way good comes from all that happens to us. So, I'm here to say about being in the standard-of-care arm of the study, "That's good!!!"

I guess it's the Tibetan version of the life attitude that supposedly drew John Lennon to Yoko Ono. The story goes that he attended an art show of hers where there was a tall ladder up to the ceiling where there was a tiny slip of paper. When you went up the ladder and read the paper, it said, "Yes!" So, in honor of John and Yoko,

I am also saying "Yes!" to standard of care treatment and to this whole experience.

Gary met me at a hotel that night, and at 8:30 A.M. on my birthday (I called that one, didn't I?!) we checked into the "infusion center" in the Cancer Center. I was to receive one drug that they drip slowly though an IV into your blood. The drug is quite amazing, really. It's called Rituxan and it's the newest, high tech drug I will receive.

It works sort of like a laser lock. The drug travels through the body and attaches to cells that have a specific target antigen, specifically my cancer cells. This alerts my own immune system to recognize and help destroy these cells. Unfortunately, it destroys other normal cells in the process, but the theory is my body can replace these.

So, they started my IV at 9:30 A.M. and unhooked me at 4:30 P.M. Unfortunately, I had a minor allergic reaction to the drug so they had to liberally use Benadryl and slow the drip way down, which is why it took all day. I do have to say Stanford showed itself to be more than a cold, clinical institution when first the nurse brought me a chocolate muffin because she knew it was my birthday, and then a man with a guitar appeared and all the nurses and orderlies gathered around and sang happy birthday to me, just like at Chevy's!

"That's good!!"

I was so happy to be back in my home, but by 9 P.M. I was running a high enough fever that the on-call emergency line doc at Stanford told me I had to go to the local emergency room to have my blood count checked.

After more sticking of veins and drawing of blood and consulting with Stanford, they decided that although my blood counts were definitely low (at least the medicine is working!), I was safe to go home, now 12:30 A.M.

All of your loving energy must be pouring out of me, because as we left, the extremely overwhelmed and obviously overworked emergency room doc actually said, "Thank you for being so nice to me!"

So here I am today—no fever and less pain. I apparently made it through step one. Next Tuesday I do the same Rituxan treatment again. On Thursday I do the four drug "cocktail". This is the one everyone thinks about when you think chemo, the one that makes you nauseous and makes your hair fall out.

"That's good!"

I will get to try out new hair-styles via wigs and experiment with cute hats and of course, most importantly, hopefully it will kill off all those malignant lymphocytes. I will essentially cycle through these treatments for the next five to six months.

Again, I can't tell you how much all of your love, support and good energy have meant to me. Yuan Miao is right, "That's good!"

I'm blessed with getting to experience true grace all around me. I wish you could all see your shining spirits as I do now, the radiant beauty all around me.

Love and gratitude,

Susan

26

How to Overcome Fear

At home Gary, Toby and I are struggling to maintain some sense of normalcy while adjusting at the same time to the changes cancer has brought into our lives. Instead of hurrying through my morning shower, dressing carefully for work in long skirts and boots, reminding Toby to remember his laptop, I am now often still sleeping when he needs to leave for school, dreaming of waves lapping at Gary and my sea kayaks on our honeymoon to Fiji 18 years ago. I'm comforted by sleeping in my favorite, hole-filled black tee shirt purchased there. "*BULA*!" it proclaims boldly, reminding me of the ebony-skinned, huge men with wide white smiles who greeted us that way at the airport before we loaded old ice chests and camping gear into our inflatable sea kayaks and headed down the coast of the island of Taveuni, sleeping in sea caves along the way. "*Bula*!" "Hello! Welcome!"—or translated into the parlance of my son's generation, "It's all good!"

That was always the best of Gary and me—off on an adventure where his outdoor resourcefulness and confidence could shine. One night we were walking across the reef, searching in the moonlight for lobsters to cook over our fire. Their eyes at the base of long antennae shone with an electric orange glow in the darkness, betraying their location.

Laughing, I splashed over the reef. "This is like a treasure hunt!" I was the spotter; Gary was the actual catcher, needing to grab them by the body so their whipping tails didn't slice his hands with their razor-sharp blades. But suddenly I saw a different movement, sinuous and winding, on the tops of the little waves washing over the reef. Some instinctual part of me recognized the movement and the telltale wide stripes of black and white, glowing in the moonlight. "Sea snake," I yelled, though my voice came out choked off with fear since I had read that these are the sixth most venomous snakes in the world.

"Oh my god, oh my god," I was repeating as I tried to walk backwards over the reef in my sloshing water shoes, slipping and falling, no longer carefully avoiding the precious coral, any systematic thinking wiped out by my terror. Out of nowhere Gary appeared by my side with a long forked stick fetched from the thick Mangrove forests lining the shore. Deftly he positioned himself between me and the snake, guided me backwards with one arm, while he lifted the banded beauty, writhing and protesting, onto his stick. Steady and sure-footed he marched down the beach and "relocated" it, flinging it far out to sea, giving me that primal sense of being protected by my man. I know, I know, not very feminist, but the truth is that I was terrified and not going anywhere near that snake. Gary, on the other hand, was fearless. Later that night, using only a tarp for a tent, suddenly overwhelmed with the reality of being alone on a tiny island in the middle of the Pacific and made aware of our mortality by the snake, we made love with the kind of passion that comes out of an awareness of the vastness of the universe and the brevity of life.

But now another stealthy invader has entered our lives, and it can't just be marched down the beach on a stick. So, in a humble effort to protect me, Gary makes the coffee and cream of wheat in the morning and reminds Toby to look at the sign by the front door, "Stop, Think," that we have placed there to help both of them in their struggles with organizational challenges caused by Attention Deficit Disorder. Artists, they prefer to live in the right sides of their brains. I used to be the one providing the executive functions of the left brain. Now, it is only the two of them, managing alone, rushing to not be late and sharing the intimacy of the half-hour car ride to school that I used to cherish. I often call Gary at work mid-day just in case there was a tidbit revealed, giving us a fleeting glimpse into Toby's world. I realize some of what I fear is the insidious way cancer is stealthily robbing me of my former life, even as I sleep.

They go off to their separate worlds, partially protected from their private fears about my cancer by the demands of other realities. A junior in high school, Toby will not only flow from Algebra to World Literature to Spanish to Art Studio, but the college counselor will also accost him with Advanced Placement Test applications and sign ups for presentations by visiting college representatives. Gary will settle into his cubicle at his job, where he will totally lose himself in his computer for eight to nine hours, working on design projects for a company whose products are all oriented toward educating investors about esoteric, niche investment opportunities. A world that has always seemed somewhat remote to me now seems like another planet.

I will stay home alone in our house, which suddenly seems empty and ridiculously large, attempting to create a new life. In the moment after my doctor's phone call, "The cells from the needle biopsy are definitely malignant," I stepped over a threshold into a parallel universe; suddenly I am in the land of sickness and, hopefully, also in the land of healing. I can still see Gary and Toby over there in our former world, and I am trying to maintain my life there, but my priorities are already rapidly shifting and the only things that seem to matter are experiencing each precious moment fully and doing the things that might help me stay alive.

Although I am regularly attending the Blue Pearl meetings during this time, I have not mentioned to anyone that I have cancer. Miao is planning to go into retreat in the mountains above San Bernardino at a place called Big Bear to revise her book, previously published in English, which is now going to be published in Chinese.

Right around the time I am to begin treatment, I receive an email from the Blue Pearl Group, "We are pleased to inform everyone that Miao will not be going to Big Bear, but instead she will remain in Mill Valley to revise her book. She will continue to join us for the Wednesday evening groups."

Not only will the Blue Pearl meetings continue, but a special four-month series called *The Vajra Wisdom Cycle: 6 Ancient Secrets for Health and Vitality and Longevity in the 21st Century* will begin. The first will be on February 28, six days after I begin my chemotherapy.

I am stunned: could this be a coincidence that now Miao will be near me, offering specific wisdom teachings as I go through my treatment? Or is Guan Shi Yin Pu Sa working her mystical magic again? I later learn that Miao had some "esoteric" experiences that influenced her to not go to Big Bear, but to stay in Mill Valley, that winter and spring.

Six days after my first chemotherapy on my birthday, I make my way through the soccer moms and yoga bodies in the parking lot of the Community Center and enter the portal to the Blue Pearl. The title of the evening's teaching is, "How to Overcome Fear." I had just written in my email to my friends, "Of course I am scared out of my mind." Miao's unearthly voice is floating through the room as she plays the harp and sings, "Blue Pearl, Blue Pearl, atop of the lotus, most precious jewel. Blue Pearl, Blue Pearl, magical power, most precious jewel." When her dark eyes meet mine, the energy is strong and clear, connected and yes, fearless.

She stands and doesn't speak, holding us in that centered silence I remember from our first meeting at Open Secret Bookstore.

"Greed," she simply states.

I'm thinking, "Aren't we supposed to be learning about letting go of fear?" Images of my own many greedy actions flashing through my mind, I am immediately cringing internally. I am the tow-headed nine-year-old in Sunday School learning that greed is one of the seven deadly sins. But Miao exudes no judgment; in fact, she is holding out an antidote.

"Letting go," she states simply. Her eyes hold the energy of the room as she obviously is waiting for us to digest the connection between these human possibilities. "Letting go of grasping is letting go of attachment. Without attachment, a natural fearlessness develops." Smiling at us, she is the kind mother, patiently nudging her eager but still uncomprehending young toward awareness.

"Remember our mantra is 'That's Good!'" she announces with enthusiasm.

"*BULA*!" I'm remembering the smiling, relaxed Fijians.

"Whatever happens, approach it openheartedly with an attitude of 'That's good.' That will help you develop fearlessness."

She is once again holding up the white cardboard with the four words scrawled in red across the back: courage, trust, faith, surrender.

Somehow we are all on our feet dancing around the room and playfully bumping into each other, then making eye contact and exclaiming, "That's good!" Walking to my car under a million diamond points of light from distant stars and planets, I feel in every cell, "That's good."

After our wedding, Gary and I traveled to Fiji.

PRACTICE

How to Overcome Fear

Day 1

Today, notice one life event that you instinctively respond to with "Oh, no!" and experiment with greeting it with an attitude of "That's good," instead. Take a few minutes to actually think of several ways good may come out of this event.

Day 2

Vajra Wind is a special practice taught by Miao based on the ancient, healing wisdom of Tibet. This Vajra Wind exercise uses simple breathing and movement to help overcome fear. It is helpful for the kidneys, which according to traditional Chinese Medicine can be negatively impacted by unmanaged fear.

Stand with feet shoulder width apart, tall but relaxed, with arms at your sides. Inhale through your nose. Cross your arms with open palms in front of your face, and slowly lower them as you squat down. As you go down, softly make the sound of "Traaaay" (rhymes with say), and maintain upper pressure on the kidneys by squeezing your anal sphincter. Fold your arms around your knees as you tuck your head. Concentrate on inhaling through your nose as you stand up, lifting your arms at your sides with palms up, to repeat the cycle. Repeat seven times.

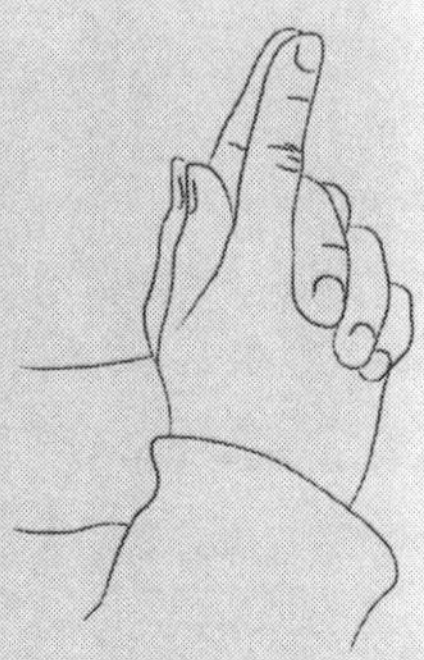

Day 3

Pyramid Mudra. Lie down on your back with legs straight, and place left foot over right ankle. (You can do this in bed at night if you have difficulty falling asleep. You can also do this sitting if you are not in a situation where you can lie down.) Clasp hands, intertwining the fingers. Extend the index fingers, touching pads together. Place thumbs side-by-side, pointing in same direction as index fingers. Rest the mudra on top of your navel area (or as an alternative position, form mudra and extend straight arms overhead). Breathe deeply and relax your muscles. Close your eyes and focus on the mudra. Take time to feel its shape. Try to sense the actual vibration associated with the shape (if you can't sense this yet, just try to open to the possibility that there is such a vibration.) Then try to sense your own energetic vibration and align it with the vibration of the mudra.

Lie quietly for at least 10 minutes and practice watching your eyeballs. (Miao says this is an ancient practice. She is not inclined to explain it with "concepts," but she emphasizes it can result in profound transformation.)

Day 4

Mantra: Ah Om Hum Hum. Sit quietly with hands resting comfortably on your thighs. Close your eyes, relax your muscles and clear your mind. Inhale through your nose as you do in the visualization of The Breath of Light. (p.65) Choose a single tone and as you exhale chant **Ah Om Hum Hum** (Ahh, Ohmm, Home, Home) in a long, slow, sustained tone, while you feel sound vibrations radiating outward and permeating every cell. Chant for at least 5 minutes.

Day 5

Color visualization. Sit quietly. Close your eyes, relax your muscles and clear your mind. Visualize the Blue Pearl: a deep blue color, cobalt blue, with a diffuse purple glow around the edges. Try to sense the vibration of these colors. Light is electromagnetic energy and each color has a different wave length, giving it a particular frequency. According to Miao, the frequencies of specific colors are beneficial for healing specific conditions of body, mind, emotions and spirit. Try to sense your own energetic vibration and align it with that of each of these colors.

Day 6

Intention. Sit quietly and take the time to formulate a clear intention for this practice. Remember, intentions are most effective if they are positive (what you DO want) and in the present tense. The intention should be your own, but an example is, "I am releasing fear as I connect with the abundance of the universe."

Day 7

Putting it all together.

Repeat the Vajra Wind exercise to help overcome fear 7 times

Lie down on your back and cross left leg over right. (Sitting is also fine.) Close your eyes, relax your muscles and breathe naturally.

Form the Pyramid Mudra

Repeat your intention slowly three times.

Visualize the Blue Pearl, a deep, cobalt blue color with a diffuse, purple glow around the edges.

While still holding the mudra, inhale using the pattern from The Breath of Light. As you exhale, chant Ah Om Hum Hum (Ahh,

Ohmm, Home, Home) as you feel the sound vibrations radiating outward from your center and permeating all of your cells. Continue for at least five minutes, increasing the amount of time as you feel comfortable.

Finish your exercise by listening to **water sounds**. Miao teaches these sounds are healing for the kidneys and good for releasing fear. (Listen to a CD of waterfalls, ocean waves or rain. If you have rain sticks gently tip them up and down.)

If you are serious about developing a practice, I suggest making a commitment to doing this exercise for 40 days.

27

Transformation at the Wig Shop

From: Susan Sattler
Date: March 4, 2007 10:59 PM
Subject: Susan Sattler's Ongoing Journey

To all my friends,

The headline news for me is that all of your love, sending of good energy and light, and nurturing support of all kinds is working its wonders because despite beginning major league chemo, I am currently doing amazingly well. Things can be different treatment to treatment, side effects can be cumulative, and I admittedly have not hit the ten-to-fourteen-day after treatment point when my white blood count levels will be at their lowest and I will be vulnerable to infection, but I am counting my blessings on a daily basis and as of today, they are many and wonderful.

So, here's the week's story. I went back to Stanford last Tuesday for another treatment of Rituxan, the laser-lock wonder drug. You may remember it targets the cancer cells so my immune system can recognize them as foreign and attack them (though I'm trying to have less warlike language for this process, so I see it more like helping them die gracefully, transform energetically and move on to another plane of existence). However, Gary did strike my analogy fancy by suggesting that the malignant lymphocytes were like the Iraqi insurgents who had gotten a hold of American uniforms early on in the war—makes it quite difficult to know whom to shoot at. (Not that we should be shooting at anyone, of course.)

Anyway, I did better with this infusion, no allergic reaction this time. I was in a lot of pain Tuesday night, but they assure me this means laser lock is working.

Grace is all around me to be sure. I arrived home to find that three of my neighbors had become house elves in our absence, cleaning, fluffing the nest, even taking our garbage to the corner for the weekly pickup. I am deeply touched by all the love and caring being extended to me. Surely, this is the best of the human spirit, and I see it literally flowing out of all your hearts.

I had prevailed upon my spontaneous, adventuresome and especially kind and supportive friend, Pam, to go off on the quest to the wig store with me. My friend Nancy had procured a name of a place said to be the only one in Santa Rosa that was not HORRIBLE, so we set off on Wednesday morning. I felt like the character in a mythical story clutching the name of a place where there was a task I must fulfill on my journey of transformation.

We traveled through the wine country on a beautiful, sunny day and arrived in a small parking lot of a tiny commercial island near the crossroad stop called Larkfield. The building was low, flat, brown, completely nondescript, and said only Elizabeth's Wig Salon on the front.

Pam and I exchanged that look you give each other before choosing voluntarily to enter into an experience which may be completely bizarre. Through another wormhole; this cancer experience seems to be filled with them. We are suddenly in the midst of every young girl's fantasy playroom, surrounded by wigs of all colors, styles and lengths, hats of velvet with beautiful beaded broaches, hats with wild Hawaiian prints, and scarves to tie in mysterious twists to give you exotic and formerly unknown looks.

In the back is a separate room that is obviously a small beauty salon. We are immediately the new girls at the event - drawn to touch and try, and simultaneously arrested by the insecurity of being in unfamiliar territory. At that moment we meet Judy, the little, round owner of the salon who has a short, middle aged, reddish-blonde curly hair style that she immediately tells us is a wig.

The universe seems to lie in wait for wonderful opportunities to present our spiritual teachers in the most capricious and surprising of disguises. Who would have expected someone who looks like Yoda to be Yoda? Judy seemed to wave a magic wand of acceptance and letting go and embracing the unknown, and we were magically swept into what can only be described as a wonderful fantasy afternoon of playing magical dress up, fearlessly letting go of old, clung-to identity and enthusiastically reaching for the next possibility.

Judy holds the deep understanding that the cancer journey requires one to fearlessly face and embrace the unknown. Then she teaches you to do that through play and fantasy and joy in creative spirit.

A dark blonde in my former life, I donned a brunette wig, placed a flower rose in my teeth, and gave Pam my most seductive smile.

"What do you think of this one?" I asked. Her uncensored laughter steered me to other choices, and I eventually selected a honey-toned bob.

Hours later, wig in bag, we departed in a definitely altered state. It was the perfect event for the afternoon preceding my first heavy-duty chemo.

Gary and I drove back to Stanford the next morning and by noon a nurse was pushing a huge, powerful Western medicine drug into my vein through a giant syringe hooked to my IV. I felt strangely calm, and a long way from Elizabeth's Wig Salon. I received three different big-time drugs over about two hours.

My nurse found out I was a psychotherapist so she spent the time telling me all about her problems with her boyfriend! We all have our gifts to offer, one of mine has always been to listen.

Then we drove home, a mercifully uneventful trip. Say many prayers of thanks to the drug companies who have developed amazingly effective anti-emetics: no throwing up yet. I feel quite spaced-out, but not sick in any way. I guess I passed another of the many challenges along this path.

Thank you to all of the wonderful cooks who have been nourishing and sustaining us as we make this journey. I cannot express in words how this helps us in all ways, emotionally, nutritionally, spiritually, mentally, everything! You are affirming all the best in the universe!

My love and deepest gratitude,

Susan

28

Who Is at the Center of the Wheel?

The next morning, having listened to Gary and Toby heading out the driveway, whizzing off to their separate worlds, I am sitting on my zafu, determined to keep my vow to do the mudra and mantra DVD every day. I am checking in to see how my body has reacted over night to powerful, toxic drugs percolating through every cell of my body. So far, so good. I am tired and somewhat spaced out, but all things considered, I feel better than I expected.

I'm remembering the odd scene from the day before in the infusion room: probably 10 cancer patients in various states of physical breakdown are sitting in leather recliners receiving infusions of chemotherapy while they watch daytime TV on their individual monitors attached to swivel arms above their heads. I'm guessing they just want to divorce themselves from what is happening to them. "Talking heads" whisk them off to Iraq, filling them with fears bigger than cancer, ESPN offers the vicarious experience of being a Super Bowl star, and reruns of *CSI: Miami* remind them life could be worse—you could be the victim of a brutal crime. I worry for them. Who is at the center of their medicine wheel? I wish the Lakota medicine man could make a surprise visit here and remind us all that *we* are in the center, we are the direction of within.

Repeating my mantra, "Courage, Trust, Faith, Surrender," I crawl onto my chair and begin to create my little tableau on the table beside me: a tiny statue of Guan Yin, a small chunk of purple amethyst geode, a white owl feather, my CD player, the CD of Miao's mantric chanting called, simply, *Love*, and a CD of Christian monks singing Gregorian chants in Notre Dame Cathedral in Paris. I try to imagine no one is noticing me as I twist my fingers into the empowerment mudra in front of my heart, pop in my ear buds and drift off, listening to the healing vibrations of mantras, manifestations of divine love.

At one point on the *Love* CD there is the sound of running water, maybe it's actually rain sticks, and I visualize the chemotherapy drugs washing through me, washing away the malignant cells and leaving my system beautifully cleansed and pristine. I repeat my mantra over and over, "All my cells are perfect." I feel calm and safe. I have befriended even the chemotherapy. I offer it to my body with love and compassion.

Now back home, I am fully committed to staying in that state. Even though I am tired from the chemotherapy, I pick up the mudra and mantra DVD. Like any finger skill (keyboarding, playing the piano, playing guitar), the mudras are becoming easier. Needing to concentrate less, I'm more able to chant the mantras myself and remember the color visualizations. As I practice, I feel a sense of harmony; I feel unified somehow, like my wheel is beginning to balance. It is a compelling feeling, reinforcing my desire to continue.

Having always felt a healing power in nature, I decide to add a long, brisk walk every day after my mudra/mantra practice. Blessed with living in the Sonoma County countryside, I can put on my shoes and just start walking down our country lane, lined with lavender and huge old live oaks. I pass the herd of white goats at the corner, the babies bleating and bounding in one leap onto the pile of hay bales in the center of their pasture. I continue past the old apple orchard where six deer munch on new grass, around the bend where a flock of wild turkeys gobble at me, the males fanning their tail feathers in colorful arcs, and head down the hill past the pond with the frogs that croak through the night.

My cells feel open, I'm literally breathing in the universe. The energizing effect of the mudra and mantra practice is palpable. As I pass under a eucalyptus grove I stretch my arms open above my head and welcome in the healing fragrance. Confronted with the possibility of death, I am intoxicated with love of life. Busy no longer defines me; my heart is not dying; in fact, it has cracked wide open.

PRACTICE

Optimizing Your Chemotherapy Experience

It can take several hours to receive an infusion. Even if you have friends, family, and healthcare workers there with you, it is something you go through alone. It is your journey. I found it essential to have many practices I could turn to for support. Here are some that were particularly helpful for me.

• Take along, and listen to, music that has a healing vibration for you.

• Visualize the chemotherapy drugs washing away the malignant cells, leaving your system beautifully cleansed and pristine. I found repeating this simple mantra at the same time was helpful, "All my cells are perfect."

• Practice the Breath of Light (p. 65) during your infusion.

• Practice the Pyramid Mudra (p. 148) while you do The Breath of Light.

• Close your eyes, relax your muscles and clear your mind. Visualize a blue orb with a diffuse purple glow surrounding it. Try to sense the vibration of each color. Light is electromagnetic energy and each color has a different wave length, giving it a particular frequency. Try to align your energetic vibration to that of each color. Enjoy visualizing these two colors while you practice the Breath of Light.

• During the infusion, close your eyes, relax your muscles, breath deeply and regularly while you visualize the Blue Pearl resting in a beautiful lotus blossom. Remembering that Miao teaches that the Blue Pearl is your perfect, essential nature and that it has magical powers, open to its miracles.

• Drink lots of water.

• Connect with nature as soon as possible. (If there is a window, look at the trees and the sky during the infusion. If you are fortunate enough to see clouds, watch them and notice how easily one form can flow into a new and completely different form - impermanence.) Immediately afterwards, if weather permits, walk around outside, focusing on nature and imagining you are drawing its powerful life force directly into your body.

• Sleep. My doctor father used to regularly say, "Sleep's the best medicine."

29

Anger, Despair, and the Internal Terrain

I am not primarily aware of anger during this time, but I am sure it is lurking deep in my subconscious. How could it not?

A life-threatening condition has come seemingly out of the blue and turned my life upside down. More importantly, I begin to realize that my unmanaged and not transformed anger about any number of things over the years may have contributed to the formation of my cancer in the first place.

There was that difficult divorce years ago. And then there were some heated meetings with teachers and school administrators as we tried to guide our son, with his unique learning style, through the bureaucratic morass of public school. There were those insurance companies denying our medical claims for no apparent reason. There was my desire to be a full-time mother, thwarted by the economic realities of modern life. And, of course, there were the daily irritations of bills not paid on time, teenagers not home on time, commitments forgotten, and on and on: concerns that seem so petty in the current reality of my life being on the line.

I know there will be those who will be thinking of Susan Sontag and her 1978 book, Illness as Metaphor, in which she challenged the "blame the victim" mentality which she felt was often embedded in the language used to describe certain illnesses and the people who suffer from them. She was particularly angry about the idea of a "cancer personality," with the associated idea that patients brought on the disease themselves.

I am certainly not blaming the victim here. I am well aware that the development of cancer is a complex process, involving both genetic and environmental factors, but I do believe excessive stress can play a role in compromising the immune system. An interesting area of current cancer research has to do with inflammation. In *Anti Cancer: A New Way of Life*, by David Servan-Schreiber, M.D., PhD, published in 2008, he comments on recent research reviewed in the journal Science:

"It has been proven that the more successful cancers are in provoking local inflammation, the more aggressive the tumor and the better it is at spreading over long distances, ultimately reaching lymph nodes and creating metastases." (p. 39). There are many studies that show our emotional state can directly contribute to actual inflammation in the body. Our emotional states can cause immediate chemical changes at the cellular level, causing production of either harmful or beneficial substances. Servan-Schreiber states, "One cause for the sudden overproduction of inflammatory substances, which is rarely mentioned when cancer is discussed, is psychological stress. Some emotional states, especially persistent anger or despair, can provoke chronic secretion of noradrenaline (known as the fight or flight hormone) and of cortisol. These hormones prepare the body for a potential wound, in part by stimulating the inflammation factors needed to repair tissues. At the same time, these hormones are also fertilizer for cancerous tumors, latent or already established." (p. 41)

When I read this, I knew I needed to think carefully about which emotional states of mine might have contributed to chronic "overproduction of inflammatory substances," especially if those substances can be "fertilizer for cancerous tumors." If I am going to heal from cancer, and then have my best chance to stay cancer free, one of the things I need to do is find a way to not experience persistent anger or hopeless despair.

I know I felt both during my first marriage. My then husband and I just could not find our way out of a destructive pattern we replayed over and over. Afraid of not living up to my expectations (which I now realize were undoubtedly unrealistic), he would lie about reality, becoming quite proficient at pretending to be whomever he thought I needed him to be. No amount of therapy seemed to help. I became chronically angry and was sinking into serious despair; that's why I finally called it quits after four years.

And then for many years I felt despair about certain aspects of my psychotherapy practice. I was missing the stimulation and creativity I felt in graduate school. The woman who gave intuitive readings described a frustrated, unhappy child constrained by the apparatus of her swing, but 17 years after that "reading" I was metaphorically still forcing myself to stay in that swing.

When my son was born, I longed to have the freedom to spend more time with him, but we needed my income. I felt trapped: I had training, I had a profession; it made sense for me to contribute financially. Besides, it only seemed fair since I knew that Gary also would love to have the luxury of staying home. I used to say, "I feel trapped by my functionality." It was sort of a joke, but underneath was certainly some growing despair, and yes, anger at Gary for not supporting me financially, and then at myself for wanting him to do that. My desire for that support certainly did not live up to my ego ideal: that I was a strong, independent, self-sufficient, equal contributor—a sterling example of feminism. Yes, there was plenty of persistent anger to go around.

Then there was Dan's suicide. A year later my mother died, and a year and a half after that, I was diagnosed with cancer.

In my search for all information that might contribute to my healing, I have come across an interesting term used by some naturopathic doctors: internal terrain. These doctors believe that the state of a person's internal environment may be more important in determining disease than the infecting organism or the pathogen itself. The condition of the internal "terrain" is directly related to the susceptibility of the individual to develop a serious illness like cancer. In addition to our physical internal terrain, there is also a complex interplay with the mental, emotional and spiritual internal terrain: something the Lakota have been representing in their medicine wheels for generations. My persistent anger and bouts with hopeless despair undoubtedly did not contribute to a healthy, well-balanced internal terrain.

30

How to Pacify Anger

"Blue Pearl, Blue Pearl, from emptiness, most precious jewel." Miao teaches that the Blue Pearl is our beautiful and perfect essential nature. She is urging us back again and again to the deepest layer wherein lies the potential for healthy internal terrain, our "inner nature."

The Blue Pearl meeting devoted to "How to Pacify Anger" begins with a lengthy meditation. Holding the "empowerment mudra" with our fingers entwined and stretched, we are connecting with powerful acupressure points and opening deep energy channels known as meridians.

The clear, reverberating sound of the Tibetan bowl Miao strikes as she moves around us brings me out of a deep and peaceful place.

"Grasping," she says.

Fortunately right now, exiting meditation, I do not feel I am grasping at anything, so I can wait peacefully to see where this is going.

"When grasping is gone, the power of other poisons—hatred, delusion, pride, suspicion—is also lessened." Holding us in her calm, focused energy, she waits, modeling the infinite capacity of the mind to be enlarged, spacious, more like the sky or the ocean.

"Out of emptiness comes abundance."

Again, she is the patient mother waiting for the young to catch on.

Her statement seems like a paradox to me. How can abundance come out of emptiness? I sit, trying to open my mind to new possibilities. My understanding is that "emptiness" does not connote nihilism. I have heard the Dalai Lama explain that all things are empty of intrinsic reality. He says that everything relies on something else for its existence. What we think of as reality is in a constant state of flux, with forms dissolving and new forms arising all the time. He says that as we deepen our insight into the ultimate nature of reality, phenomena and events will seem sort of illusory or illusion-like. When we fully experience the emptiness of phenomena we are no longer locked into a limited idea of a static reality. We can connect with the limitless potential in the universe. When we open to the underlying energy of all creation, from which all things are made, abundance is obvious because there is constantly new creation.

So I think I am beginning to get it. Grasping comes from a belief in limited resources: what we see is what we have, and I had better hold onto whatever I have or I risk having nothing. Some psychologists refer to this as coming from a place of scarcity.

If I hold this belief, I am in danger of hating (or at least being angry at) anyone who tries (or might try) to take what I have, or who seems to have more than I do. Suspicion, delusion, pride and envy would be likely to arise as fall-out from this belief system as well. However, if I know that the universe is infinitely abundant, constantly creating, there is no need for grasping. I can more easily let go of my attachments, knowing something new will arise to take their place.

I am unable to pursue these thoughts further, because Miao is speaking again.

"Ego. When you overcome ego you can be in the divine wrathful."

Now I am moving out of my complacent, comfortable post-meditative state. I'm not sure yet what she means by the "divine wrathful," but

I certainly know about ego. Yes, there is definitely some work for me to do here. And even in my infant state of spiritual development, I can see the relationship between ego and anger. Ego is the part of my psyche that allows me to experience myself as a separate, distinct individual and to have consciousness of my own identity. A healthy ego can contribute to healthy self-esteem, but when things are out of balance, ego can create an inflated sense of superiority to others. Unchecked ego wants to believe it is always right (since it knows more than anyone else); and for confirmation of this, it depends on external validation. When overwhelmed with ego, I am easily angered by anyone who does not agree with me, and especially by those who seem to criticize me, because my ego feels threatened.

I still cringe when I think of an incident that happened when I was first teaching high school. You'll remember that I was charged with the task of implementing a comprehensive women's sports program for the school when Title IX was passed into law, requiring equal opportunity for young women and men. As you might imagine, this was no easy task. The men's program had to share everything that had previously been theirs alone: budgets, staff, facilities, and transportation. A whole infrastructure for the new program had to be created—leagues, coaches, game schedules, uniforms, everything.

I worked incredibly hard on this for months and was very proud of the result. The local newspaper came to one of our first league volleyball games and interviewed me before the game. The reporter wanted to know all about Title IX. I went on and on about how there had been no program or opportunity for girls in this school before this fabulous program that now existed. I thought my intent was to validate the importance and effectiveness of Title IX. When I arrived at school the day after the story appeared in the newspaper, the male athletic director pulled me aside saying, "I need to talk with you about a certain article in the newspaper, and the effect of blowing your own horn." I was instantly enraged.

"Blowing my own horn? How about just telling the truth about how things really were for girls all these years? There was nothing for them before Title IX made equal opportunity a law and this program became possible."

"Well, that's not exactly how Mrs. Peterson and I see it. We spent a lot of hours setting up the Girls' Athletic Association and a lot of years providing activities for girls before you got here."

"The Girls' Athletic Association? You mean that *club* for girls who were athletic? That *club* that provided maybe three little play games with another school for a couple of sports?" I was flooded with stress hormones: my face was hot and my heart was beating wildly. How dare him imply that their little club stood a candle to what these girls had now! (What I created, my ego was adding.) How could he not be praising me up and down for what I had done?

"You'll understand one day that we all stand on the shoulders of others who came before us, and we always need to acknowledge what they did."

I was furious for days. I fantasized quitting. "So fine," my ego said. "You think you can keep all this going without me, you'll see." I felt like Nixon, "You won't have Susan Sattler to kick around anymore." But of course I didn't leave, and I eventually realized that he was right. I'm still embarrassed when I think about my young arrogance. We all make our contribution and hopefully together we move things incrementally forward. My ego was so fully invested I hadn't given a thought to what others had done before me. The reality was that I was just part of an ongoing continuum.

My ego is like that, clever and slippery, with the ability to slide onto the stage like a well-practiced con artist. I am often the last to notice that it has entered, stage left, and taken over the show. I certainly hadn't noticed it as I happily "blew my own horn" with that reporter. As I'm musing about how to keep tabs on my wily ego, which generates outrage, arrogance and anger, Miao slips us the answer.

"Awareness is the Divine Fire Department which can immediately put out anger."

Hearing these words, I feel a kind of relief spread over me. I know I can't just voluntarily drop my ego, but Miao seems to be saying that we can use awareness to notice when it is unhealthily engaged, and to observe how much of our anger and suffering are the result of its needs. It makes sense that as our understanding of this cause of suffering increases, ego dissolves.

Her eyes alight with awareness, Miao emphasizes another kind of energy.

"The divine wrathful allows us to be on fire in another way: passionate, with our passion burning away obstacles."

I'm still not so sure I understand this "divine wrathful energy," but I do have a basic understanding of passion. Unlike ego, passion is not about craving positive reflection from some external source; it is about being inspired by unrestrained, powerful feelings arising from our core. I feel passionate about my son. I would be the proverbial mother who would lift the Volkswagon to save him if he were trapped underneath. Nothing would stop me; I would be terrifying in my ability to blast through obstacles. The energy would not be anger fueled by ego, it would be pure passion arising from pin-point intention.

Absorbed in a visualization of me easily holding the front end of this Volkswagon off the ground, imagining adrenalin coursing through my body, I'm startled to hear Miao's voice. Opening my eyes, I see a fire burning in hers. "Divine wrathful energy can transform the energy of negative emotions like hatred and envy into something positive." I write this down in my journal, realizing I don't fully understand it, and I will have to do some more thinking about it later.

Her parting lesson is that wrathful energy needs to come through the central channel, not the liver, to be transformative, as opposed to harmful. My yoga teacher has explained that this channel, including the seven centers of intense energetic activity known as the chakras, is the central pathway for the subtle energies of our being. In traditional Chinese medicine, emotions and physical health are intimately connected. Organ systems are believed to be part of a complex, holistic body system, so an emotion can have extensive physical effects, especially on the organs. It is believed that irritability and inappropriate anger, for example, can be harmful to the liver. Miao seems to be saying that these negative effects are avoided when we combine awareness and intention to consciously direct "wrathful energy."

Consumed with these thoughts, I take the rose a woman is handing out as our meeting ends, and I silently walk down the stairs. Across the lobby, I hear the rhythmic thump, thump, thump from the exercise class. Kid Rock's "I'm a fist of rage, I'm a fist of rage," blares from the speaker. Remembering Miao's warning about wrathful energy, I send a silent prayer that the students' energy is flowing only through their central channels and not through their livers.

Arriving back home I am too energized to sleep. I pull out my journal and read Miao's words. "Divine wrathful energy can transform the energy of negative emotions like hatred and envy into something positive." What does this mean? I sense that I need to understand how this works. I have no doubt that persistent anger contributes to inflammation, and Servan-Schreiber tells me that in terms of cancer, the more inflammation, the more aggressive the tumor. I'm human; I'm going to experience anger, but Miao seems to be saying there is a way I could use that very energy for something positive.

As I'm researching "wrathful energy," Gary comes up behind me.

"I guess the Blue Pearl Group got you thinking about something. What's up?"

"Well, Miao made this statement tonight … Here, take a look. I wrote it in my journal."

"Hmmm," he says thoughtfully. "It's a little confusing, because when I think of wrathful, I think of angry."

"I know, but I think that may be a translation difficulty. What I've been reading suggests that wrathful is intended to suggest forceful energy—energy that can burn away obstacles, but I think the idea is a more pure energy that doesn't carry the judgments that are often associated with anger, or the emotional attachments, or the sort of lack of discipline of rageful states. I don't really know; I'm just trying to figure it out."

He's smiling. "From what you've told me about Miao, this may be one of those things you can't figure out with your brain. Doesn't she say, 'No concepts!? You may have to just let your expanded mind open to understanding over time."

Interesting. I feel some instant irritation. "I may not have time to just wait for my 'expanded mind' to magically come up with some understanding. I have cancer, remember?"

I instantly regret my words. I see the cloud of hurt cross his face. "I'm sorry," I say as quickly as possible. "See, if I were evolved enough to use wrathful energy to transform my negative emotions I could have done something different there." He gives me a forgiving smile. "But I want to figure it out," I continue. "I think it could be an essential key to my healing. I really do appreciate your being willing to talk about this stuff with me."

"And I'm honestly interested," he assures me, "but these are challenging ideas to understand, and Miao is trying to both find words to describe complicated metaphysical and mystical beliefs, and then translate those words into English. But, blasting through those obstacles, what do you already know about all this?"

"Well, if I accept what the Dalai Lama says, that all things are empty of intrinsic reality, it would follow that the energy of our emotions has no inherent existence. Like all phenomena it must be empty of intrinsic reality: it relies on something else for its existence."

"And the something else is?"

"I'm not sure. Theoretically, energy is neutral; it is only as it is acted on by our intention and resulting actions that it takes shape. Miao says awareness is the Divine Fire Department that puts out anger. Maybe with practiced awareness we notice immediately that we have aroused energy, but rather than just letting it become destructive anger we can choose to use it in another way: as passion, to achieve something positive."

My mind is racing ahead. "I think maybe we could use the wrathful energy to help us not indulge in more destructive emotions like hate and envy and maybe even to keep our ego in line—kind of like the good parent saying, "No, this stops here. We aren't going there; we have more important things to do with this energy."

Gary looks thoughtful. "Why don't you just send an email to Fay (Miao's assistant) asking if Miao could offer some clarification."

The next night we receive this response.

> "Miao said to give you a metaphor of 'Divine wrathful.' A doctor will do surgery (or an operation) on a patient if the organ or any part of the body is causing the patient to be sick or dying. After surgery the patient will be weaker or might get side effects or other unexpected results. But the surgery is necessary to save the life.
>
> "In the spiritual path, the teacher, like the doctor, in order to heal the student who is 'sick,' cuts off the disease, but with compassion and love. Then the student can go forward smoothly."

Gary raises his eyebrows. "I think you've actually been doing this, Susan. When you got the cancer diagnosis you could have been overwhelmed with anger or self-pity or envy of everyone who is healthy. This would be the 'sick' parts in a spiritual sense. But even though you are forceful about your course of action, it seems like you've been acting with compassion and love toward yourself."

"Well, I certainly feel absolutely focused. From the first moment I heard the diagnosis, I've felt like, 'No, you have the wrong girl. I will not be dying. I still have too many things to do in life.' I know there are a lot of forces involved here, and that many who have a strong will to live may die anyway, but I feel like my best shot is to be laser-focused on healing. That requires eliminating anything that does not promote my health. Raging at fate, envying others, or being overwhelmed by grief seem like distractions I don't have time for right now. I do feel consumed with a kind of forceful energy, a passion to heal and stay alive that seems to be burning through obstacles. And the motivation is certainly loving: whatever is being 'cut out' is only so I can 'go forward smoothly.'"

Gary pauses, "I'm thinking that maybe we can learn to use wrathful energy both with ourselves *and* with others, but I am sure the key is to do it without judgment, because otherwise it is just more destructive anger."

I'm suddenly aware of the dark circles under his eyes. He'll be getting up at 6:00 a.m. and going to work tomorrow. It would be completely understandable if he were saying, "This is ridiculous. I can't be staying up until all hours having philosophical conversations with you. This is a waste of time." But instead, here he is, modeling an attitude of true compassion and no judgment.

"We need to go to bed." I say softly. "I love you. That night we met when you came to the dinner at my house, I felt some kind of instant recognition. This is it, you are my teacher."

PRACTICE

How to Release Anger

Day 1

The Dalai Lama says, "Anger is like a fisherman's hook. It is very important to ensure we are not caught by it." Today, imagine you are a wily trout on the lookout for the hook of anger. When you see the hook, avoid biting on it immediately. Take a few seconds to consider what might be fueling your anger. Are you grasping onto something? Is your ego engaged? Then decide if biting on the hook of anger is going to achieve the results you really want. Maybe you'll decide to just swim away.

Day 2

Vajra Wind. This Vajra Wind exercise uses simple breathing and movement to help release anger. It is helpful for the liver, which according to Traditional Chinese Medicine can be negatively impacted by unresolved anger. Stand with feet shoulder width apart, tall but relaxed, with arms at your sides. Inhale through your nose as you slowly lift your arms, palms facing up until they meet over your head. Slowly lower hands with palms together in front of face to prayer position in front of your heart, while you forcefully make

a Shhhhh sound (the sound of "be quiet"). Eyes are held wide open to release toxins with the breath. Repeat seven times.

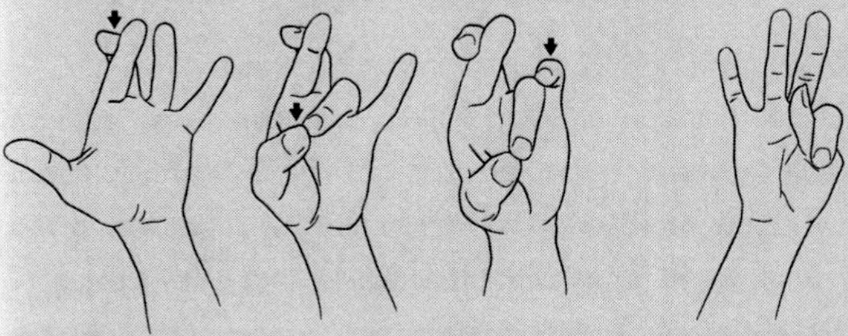

Day 3

Mudra. Releasing Anger and Blood Pressure Regulating Mudra.

Left hand: Cross fingers like for good luck (middle finger over index finger).

Touch thumb nail to tip of ring finger.

Place little finger (pinky) on top of bent knuckle of ring finger.

Right hand: Lay index finger over the top of thumb, slightly lift middle, ring and pinky.

Hold left hand in front of navel area, palm up. Place right hand in front of heart center with fingers pointing up.

Practice forming and releasing mudra until you feel comfortable. Take a deep breath and relax your muscles. Close your eyes and focus on the mudra. Take time to feel its shape. Try to sense the actual vibration associated with the shape (if you can't sense this yet, just try to open to the possibility that there is such a vibration.) Then try to align your own energetic vibration with the vibration of the mudra.

Day 4

Mantra: Namo Nan Gala Om Ah Hum. Sit quietly. Close your eyes, relax your muscles and clear your mind. Inhale through your nose using the visualization from The Breath of Light. (p. 65) As you exhale, chant **Namo Nan Gala Om Ah Hum** (Nahmoh, Nahn Gahlah Ohm Ahh Home) in a long, slow, sustained tone, while you imagine sound and white light energy radiating outward and permeating every cell. Chant for at least five minutes.

Day 5

Color visualization. Sit quietly. Close your eyes, relax your muscles and clear your mind. Visualize the colors sepia (a light brown like in old fashioned photographs), purple, and light yellow. Try to sense the vibration of each color. Light is electromagnetic energy and each color has a different wave length, giving it a particular frequency. Try to sense your own energetic vibration and align it with that of each color.

Day 6

Intention. Sit quietly and take the time to formulate a clear intention for this practice. Remember, intentions are most effective if they are positive (what you DO want) and in the present tense. The intention should be your own, but an example is, "I am releasing anger and filling myself with the healing energy of love."

Day 7

Putting it all together

Repeat the Vajra Wind exercise for releasing anger seven times.

Sit quietly. Close your eyes, relax your muscles and breathe naturally.

Form the Releasing Anger and Blood Pressure Regulating Mudra.

Focus on your intention.

Visualize the colors **sepia, purple and light yellow**.

Inhale using the visualization from The Breath of Light. As you exhale, chant Namo Nan Gala Om Ah Hum and feel the sound vibration radiating outward from your center, permeating all of your cells.

Continue for at least five minutes, increasing the amount of time as you feel comfortable.

Finish your exercise by listening to **wood sounds**. Miao teaches these sounds are healing for the liver and good for releasing anger. (Gently tap two wooden drumsticks, shake wooden Maracas, play a wooden flute.)

31

Burning Strands of Hair

From: **Susan Sattler**
Date: **March 27, 2007 10:15 PM**
Subject: **Susan's Still Out Here!**

Hi my good energy friends!

I know I sort of dropped off the map for a few weeks here. After weeks of preparation, planning my route, gathering of information, and being embraced in a golden net of love and support from well-wishers, I've finally fully embarked on my journey.

As you know, after the first full round of chemo, I did remarkably well: little nausea, pretty good energy, great attitude. I felt like the captain of the ship finally unfurling the sail, letting the sea air blow through my hair, looking out to an unbroken horizon stretching before me. I was ready to take on whatever might be coming.

By day fourteen after the chemo, as I would run my fingers through my hair they would come forth trailing strands of golden hair which would drift away on the breeze in the sun. I thought the strands were actually quite beautiful, and I also knew this was the beginning of my next lesson in letting go: letting go of more strands of former identity.

I knew I would lose my hair on this journey, but I was uncertain of how, exactly, that process happened. Did you just wake up one morning with it all in a pile on your pillow? Did you take a shower one day and watch it all run off your head and down the drain? As I probably could have imagined, the process for me has mirrored the way I seem to let go of other things in my life—a few strands at a time, feeling nostalgic, trying to remember and honor the value and still let go.

Each day, I let go of more and more handfuls of hair; I began carrying a paper bag around and filling it, twirling the hair into a nest-like pattern. It brought back flashes of memory of the birds' nests we would find as children in our South Dakota paradise with our horses' hair carefully woven into the center.

By the sixth day I had only odd, wild wisps of hair tenaciously hanging on. My neighbor, Sheila, called it exactly when she said I had that "feral look," like small children who run wild through fields of grass, exactly what I did look like as a little girl: a flash of wild, blonde wisps of oh-too-fine hair. This cancer seems to be taking me back through time—a regression of sorts in the interest of new birth.

I realized then that the next day was the vernal equinox, that lovely balance point when we begin to let go of the old to make room for the new, a celebration of renewal and rebirth, a time of connecting with nature's miraculous ability to renew itself. My second full-on chemo would be the following day, the first full day of spring!

I knew exactly what I wanted to do with my hair. I called my neighbor Jeannie, who has an outdoor fire pit, a beautiful garden, and a love of ritual. I needed to burn my hair.

Eight of my dear neighbors and friends gathered spontaneously at sunset for what I can only describe as a sacred ceremony. They came bearing symbolic offerings to burn with metaphoric meaning: recently pruned plants with special characteristics like endurance, peace, victory, a recently shed snakeskin, hot dried peppers from last year's garden, a dead birch branch which had broken off the tree just where a new bud was forming, white sage gathered during a Native American ritual, rose petals embodying another's journey of letting go.

I burned my hair on the eve of my second chemo, and vowed my intention to let go of fear, fear of the future, judgments and trying to control outcome. After the letting go there was an offering of seeds for the future.

The next day my friend Marg appeared at 6:30 A.M. and within hours I was back in the infusion room at Stanford with the nurse, the IV, and the huge syringes of red drugs. It was the first day I actually wore the wig, "That's good!" Everyone says I look young and healthy!! One irony is that what I have become famous for in the infusion room is my apparently "great veins." Nurses arrive saying, "Oh, you're the one, I heard about your great veins!!" You never know what your assets may be in a new culture!! "That's good!" I have blue ribbon veins!

Since chemo two I have been more nauseous, not sick, just uncomfortably queasy. The drugs also make it difficult to think. I now officially cannot keep track of my cats' names, so do not be alarmed if I call you Ink Spot.

There seem to be unending lessons of letting go. Gary and Toby have gone off to the East Coast on a rite of passage: the junior- year spring break college tour. I was determined not to miss it, but in the end acknowledged that I would be at my lowest blood levels, and airplane air and crowds were a risk I couldn't take. If I get an infection, I end up in the hospital on IV antibiotics—couldn't see myself there in someplace like Connecticut or New York City!

So, I'm here at home thinking once again of how very fortunate I am to be held in such a loving community. I know deep in my heart that I am doing well because of the care and support you all are continuing to selflessly offer to us. I cannot imagine how we would get through this without you holding us afloat in all ways.

Love and gratitude,

Susan

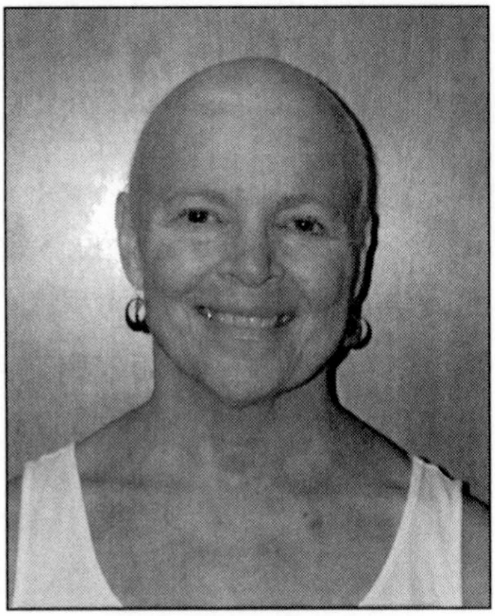

Shortly after my chemotherapy treatment began, all my hair fell out.

32

How to Find Peace and Joy and Relieve Stress

My dark blond wig is sliding off my now bald head like grease on a Teflon pan, hanging crazily to one side as I sneak an embarrassed look into the unforgiving full-length mirrors at the front of the yoga studio. Continuing the miraculous string of "coincidences" that have been occurring throughout my cancer diagnosis and treatment, Miao's assistant and devoted student, Fay, is teaching a class called The Yoga of Joy, created by Yuan Miao. The class, which is being taught in Northern California for the first time, began three days after my first chemotherapy treatment.

I still have told no one in the group of my cancer diagnosis. I feel vulnerable and private; I am still trying to integrate the reality of my diagnosis into my identity. My fear is that suddenly I will only be seen as "the cancer patient." Cancer is such a loaded word; it threatens to overwhelm everything else. So it is perfect that I am in a yoga class.

Yoga is a Sanskrit word referring to union or oneness. In her book, Miao reveals that the Yoga of Joy emanated from a deep place within her when, through the blessing of direct connection with higher states of consciousness, she spontaneously experienced naturally revealed postures and body mudras. This yoga includes elements of Tibetan tantric yoga and primordial yoga which date back 7,000 years. It is an integrated practice of visualization, breath work, physical postures, mudras, and mantras. Coming out of the Vajrayana tradition, this yoga includes not only postures and movements, but also "inward contemplation aimed toward entering empty-naturedness to enable a higher realization and growth of awareness."

A group of about eight of us are awkwardly twining our fingers into the lotus mudra, tentatively joining our voices in mantric chanting, attempting unusual body postures (actually full body mudras) and then gratefully settling into breathing practices, guided visualizations and meditation. We form the final pose, the Left Lying Sailboat position. I am lying on my left side; my arms are stretched overhead holding the pyramid mudra. My bottom leg is straight, the top leg bent so my knee comes close to my forehead.

I hear Fay's voice drifting over me, "*Yeshe Tsuomo* is a Tibetan phrase meaning 'ocean of wisdom.' A crystalline water drop merges into the great ocean and is no longer seen. This is the state of *Yeshe Tsuomu.* A tiny boat sets sail upon the sea of wisdom, leaving behind affliction and dread. It is free and self-determined, tasting the quietude of mind and body."

How different it is to think of being adrift in this way. When I wandered in to Open Secret Bookstore, reeling from my client's suicide, feeling adrift was a very scary thing. After my mother died, we were distressed at feeling adrift, in a boat with no oars. Now, I begin to experience the peace and tranquility of letting my little boat carry me away from "affliction and dread." My former external life has been falling away, but that has allowed the opening of this space where I can be more "free and self determined." I do feel lighter, relieved somehow of the pressures of daily life; yes, I would have to admit I feel a deep sense of peace and joy. Rolling up my Blue Pearl-colored yoga mat, I make a commitment to add the Yoga of Joy to my daily routine, at least until the end of my chemotherapy treatment.

In the Blue Pearl room on the following Wednesday night, we float in the heart of the community center activity. We are intent on connecting to our own hearts, similarly buried deep within our individual mundane life activity.

"Connect to the divine vibration," Miao is urging, as she moves around the room. Deep, guttural mantric sounds emanating from her transition seamlessly to beautiful, harmonic, unearthly vibrations. Periodically, she stops singing and fixes us with her vast, unwavering stare.

"Feel the vibration."

Though this vibration is palpable and undeniable in her presence, and an immediate ticket to joy, I'm imagining trying to explain this "vibration" to my medically-oriented family, or really, to many people who would be instantly recalling the Beach Boys' song, "Good, good, goo-oo-ood vibration." I'm thinking of the little crystal store in my northern California town, still run by a true hippy left over from the onslaught of '60s youth who flocked to this area as they fled urban disappointments and trauma, trying to "go back to the land" and connect to the "vibration" of the country.

But we definitely are responsive to vibration. Most of us have had the experience of being significantly affected by music. As I directly experience the obvious shift in my mood and sense of energy after listening to Miao's mantric singing, I am determined to find a way to communicate about this to others.

Two days later, a package arrives in the mail from my mother's long-time friend who is in her fourth year of remission from non-Hodgkin's lymphoma. Having spent most of her adult life in the small South Dakota town where I grew up and now in her mid-seventies, this woman was never a hippy. However, I do remember her as someone always open to new ideas and interested in cutting-edge information.

As I stand at the end of our long, country lane and let the brown wrapping fall to the ground by my mailbox, I stare at the cover of a book: *The Healing Power of Sound, Recovery from Life-Threatening Illness*

Using Sound, Voice and Music. The author, Mitchell L. Gaynor, M.D., is the former Director of Medical Oncology at the renowned Strang Cancer Prevention Center where he still serves as a consultant. The liner notes tell me he practices complementary medicine, blending traditional western treatment with complementary therapies that include nutritional supplements of herbs as well as regular visits to acupuncturists and energy healers. Still standing at the mailbox, I leaf through the book and on page 26 my eyes stop on the following: "It would not be an exaggeration to say that the synergistic effect of the singing bowls (Tibetan) and voice tones when used in combination with meditation and guided imagery has revolutionized my practice. I believe that sound, the most underutilized and least appreciated mind-body tool, should become a part of every healer's medical bag ..." Continuing to glance through the book, I notice study after study he shares showing the positive effects of sound on the immune system and all the cells, tissues and organs of the body. East meets West, and my experience of the positive benefits of mantra is externally validated.

"*Om Mani Padme Hum.*" I vibrate my way along the lane lined with English lavender back to my house, thanking Yuan Miao for the "secret" of the mantras I can use to feel peace and joy and counter the negative effects of stress in my life.

The phone is ringing as I enter the house. "Hi, Sue, it's Ann. How are you feeling?"

"Actually pretty good. I just walked down to the mailbox and discovered Joyce sent what looks like a really interesting book called *The Healing Power of Sound, Recovery from Life Threatening Illness Using Sound, Voice and Music.*"

There was an uncharacteristic pause. "That's amazing. I was just calling to tell you about the story the pastor told at church today about Jesus' disciple Paul who wrote a letter to the Ephysians—you know, they were new and potential converts to the fledgling Christian churches that were just beginning to form back then. In the letter, Paul reminds them to be compassionate, love their neighbors as themselves, be forgiving, and then he adds, 'And don't forget to sing.' Our pastor was musing on why Paul felt it was important to remind them to sing."

"Remember in Sunday School we often heard that phrase, 'Make a joyful noise unto the Lord.'"

"Right, I think that was from the Psalms. Well, anyway, my cell's almost out of batteries. I'll call you back later, but don't forget to sing!"

I sat down to think about why Paul felt it was important to remind them to sing. I suspect he understood that one of the ways to connect with divine energy was through sound, through vibration, and that it would be much more likely for these spiritual practitioners to succeed at being loving and compassionate if they were in "the vibration." I think he may also have understood that one of the best ways to glorify the great gift of life is to enjoy it, to be joyful, to "make a joyful noise unto the Lord."

Later when she called back, my sister said her minister went on to say some people don't like to sing because they don't think they sing well, and some people don't know many songs. He then made the metaphoric leap to say that the world might be improved if we made the effort to learn each others' songs: another way to find peace and joy and relieve stress.

Once again my Eastern and Western lineages are twining themselves around each other. It is clear that love and compassion are the common goal and either Alleluja or *Om Mani Padme Hum* might get us there.

Miao radiates peace and joy.

33

Stormy Seas

From: **Susan Sattler**
Date: **April 24, 2007 8:11 PM**
Subject: **Susan Hits Stormy Seas**

Hi Everyone,

Well, the ship hit stormy seas after the third chemo. I know it's been a long time since the last email. It's very difficult to write when rolling over thirty foot swells with lightning flashing over head, threatening to split the mast, and the wind howling all around you. I've been busy just trying to not let myself or any of my crew wash overboard. Hardest of all have been the solo watches when I wonder how long the storm will last. Will it get worse? And most scary of all, how many more storms will there be before port, and do I have the stamina to ride them out? Did I choose the right route; was there an easier course?

Then there are the existential questions. What is this journey all about anyway? Why am I on this particular path?

So much for metaphor for now. For the first time, I was actually sick (yes, vomiting) the night I arrived home from chemo three. Then followed twelve days when I felt terrible. It's a very difficult thing to describe since, for me, I cannot compare it to any other known experience.

It feels like none of my regulatory systems are functioning correctly, so my entire being is alien and all the warning systems are going off signaling distress. It reminds me of the old Star Trek show on TV when something went wrong with the Enterprise (the mother ship, as you remember); they had been hit by enemy Klingon fire or there was a systems failure and all kinds of lights flashed and bells rang and we knew there were only minutes to do something or the ship would blow up or plunge powerless through space. My inner Captain Kirk is frantically trying to fix the problem, but nothing seems to bring things back to normal. So, like the ship metaphor, the only thing left is to ride out the storm.

So, I have to smile as I realize this is what brings me back to transformation, and I realize I don't achieve it with a single ceremony of burning hair and making vows, although that was undoubtedly an important first step. The loss of my hair was so simple, really, in comparison to the truly big letting-goes I'm facing now.

I vowed to let go of fear, fear of the future, judgments and trying to control outcome, heady stuff - easy in a way to vow - tougher when on that night watch alone listening to the wind howl. How exactly does one let go of fear?

Yuan Miao has been talking about trust and surrender. My sixteen-year old boy Buddha who needs me as his ride along as he learns to drive has point blank told me, "You have no trust!" as I cringe and cling to the door handle. All this has made me think a lot about trust.

What does one trust if trying to let go of fear?

My family historical roots spiral back through the idyllic green cornfields of South Dakota (where we spent long, lazy childhood days on our horses riding through the irrigation sprinklers) to the barren, bleak days of the dust bowl. Both my parents came of age in that time when crops failed, banks failed and there was not much to trust except one's own ingenuity and ability to work hard. Working hard was what saved them, and gave my sister and me our secure, cocoon-like childhood.

I internalized trusting hard work, working hard as a way to be safe in the world. Really, it's a way to change things. If things are not as I like, I can work hard and change them. It works, to a point.

I first found out the limitations of this method of trying to control outcome when I was pregnant and in labor for fifty hours. The longest, scariest, most difficult part was when there was really nothing I could do but surrender—there's that other word! I had to stop working (in fact the working got in the way) and trust some power greater than myself to accomplish this miraculous transformation, this giving of new life. I truly was only the vehicle.

So here I am once again at the gate of new birth, only this time it is my own rebirth. I find myself with a knee-jerk reaction to work hard; there must be something I can do to change how I feel, to be able to skip this uncomfortable, scary, out-of-control part. But I'm sure this is part of the lesson - to trust and surrender and ride over the waves.

One element of the transformation is to develop more flexibility: there are times to work hard, and there are times to let go and trust, maybe even embrace the out-of-control ride, maybe even find a thrill in the unpredictability. Who knows where it may take me. This reminds me of John Muir, who loved nothing more than a huge storm in the Sierras. The story goes that he would lash himself to the highest tree branch where he would be whipped around wildly in the wind, laughing and thrilled.

My quest is not only to find a way through my cancer treatment, but also to allow it to carry me to a new, ever-more-conscious way of being in the world. I'm certain that my way of "working hard" to be safe in the world paradoxically exhausted me over the years, ground down my immune system, and left me vulnerable to the opportunistic lymphoma. I need to practice a new, more joyful, trusting way of taking life's ride. I have spiritual teachers all around to help.

My ever-insightful neighbor Sheila (who actually had her truck filled with our week's garbage—there's a metaphor for you) waved her fairy wand as she was leaving and cautioned me, "Don't forget to leave room for magic." Ah, yes, alchemy: perhaps an expanded example of transformation.

It is now day fourteen and I am doing better. My next chemo is in seven days, May 2nd. There truly is already magic all around me. To be so loved and cared for in so many ways is to experience the grace of the universe every moment. I'll be lashing myself to the mast on May 2nd in honor of John Muir, and holding you all in my heart as I try to embrace the ride.

Much love and gratitude,

Susan

34

One Divine Lineage

Between chemotherapy treatments, on days when I am home alone recovering, my own question is insistent. "What does one trust when letting go of fear?"

On a rainy April morning, I am on my zafu, noticing that new leaf buds are just appearing on the birch tree outside my window. With time and space to think, I'm feeling grateful for all the wisdom traditions passed down through generations of seekers in vastly different cultures. I have been offered multiple possibilities for connection with the highest potential in the universe: through the example of Jesus, the love of the Great Spirit, and the pure essence of the Blue Pearl. Woven together I see that at their core, they are the same, they form a divine lineage, the lineage of love.

I believe all three lineages are teaching that we all have perfection at our core, we only have to "remember" who we are. I have heard Miao say, "I'm not a teacher, I am a reminder." Jesus, Miao, and the Lakota medicine man can all be "reminders" to me of our greatest potential.

Miao also says, "You are so much bigger than your self." I suspect that it is something about that part that is "so much bigger," that holds the key to what I can trust when letting go of fear.

Stretching out on the living room carpet and listening to the sound of rain on the roof, I'm thinking that separate religions and different traditions have their own rituals and practices, but at their best, they are in the service of the same thing: connection to the experience of unity and wholeness where love, compassion, forgiveness and joy arise naturally. For a moment I have a glimmer of understanding that courage, trust, faith and surrender are not only necessary for full connection with this experience of unity, but they also are natural results of being in that consciousness.

I pull out Miao's DVD, thinking it's time to do my practices, but my mind seems to be on a roll about these lineages. I'm realizing that mudras show up in all three. I've never thought about this before. My revelation is causing me to sit bolt upright. Christians do mudras! They hold their hands in the prayer position. I've heard that bringing the left hand, representing the past, and the right hand, representing the future, together in the middle, symbolizes being in the present moment, right where it's optimal to be if you want to connect with a higher state of consciousness.

A graphic image of Christ hanging from the cross, nails through each hand, flashes into my mind. Our protestant church only used the bare cross as a symbol, but on Christmas Eve my family sometimes attended the midnight mass at the chapel that was part of the Catholic convent whose Benedictine Sisters served Sacred Heart Hospital where my dad saw patients. My sister and I especially looked forward to this Christmas Eve mass because it was so filled with mystery and ritual: the priests entered wearing ornate robes and swinging large incense censers. They spoke in Latin and the congregation periodically participated in hand movements everyone but us seemed to know.

This is where I remember seeing what I now know is a crucifix, a large, three-dimensional cross with a representation of Jesus' body hanging on it. At the time, only familiar with the bare cross, I was disturbed by this image. Now, deeply interested in the idea of mudra, I'm intrigued. It's suddenly obvious to me that Christ on the cross is a full body mudra, but what is the simple, energetic communication? I hold the image in my mind and wait. Sure enough, two experiences slowly well up from deep within me and translate themselves into words: suffering as an ultimate expression of compassion, and surrender. I suddenly remember reading that two of the final things Christ said on the cross were, "Forgive them Father, for they know not what they do," and "Unto you I commend my spirit."

My mind is racing now. I'm remembering watching the Catholics at those Christmas Eve masses, crossing themselves from forehead to heart and then from left shoulder to right shoulder: another mudra. Could the touching head and then heart indicate mind surrendered to heart? I've heard that left can represent the material world and right the spiritual. Could this left to right action be a mudra of material surrendered to spiritual? I know that theologians have studied these things for centuries and that they undoubtedly have complex academic understanding of these rituals, but I'm excited to feel I am receiving some kind of simple, direct communication through symbol.

By now, I have my journal out. I have written MUDRAS in large letters across the top of the page, and I am writing as fast as I can. "Native Americans form the circle, reminding us of the unity of all that is. Blue Pearl practitioners form Joyful Mudra with thumb touching index finger, also forming a circle. Miao has explained to me that the Empowerment Mudra is about more than physical health, it recreates a shape manifested in ancient times when yogis were in a state of enlightenment." Trying to get my ideas down quickly, I begin writing short phrases, "Hands in prayer, Christ on cross, sign of the cross, kneeling, tranquil mudra, snow lotus mudra, medicine wheel...."

Pausing, I glance back at the DVD, and this time the word mantra attracts my attention. If all of these lineages utilize mudras as a way to connect with higher states of consciousness, they undoubtedly all also use mantra. I'm writing, "Allelujah, Thy Will Be Done, *Mitakuye Oyasin*, and *Om Mani Padme Hum*."

Sitting back and slowing my mind, I'm trying to integrate all of this. These mudras and mantras are universal ways to connect with divine energy. The connection is possible because they carry a vibration which is simpler, more direct than speech. They all seem to be connecting us to the same source. I suddenly perceive a whole new level of unity, like arriving on a high vantage point in the mountains and realizing that the valleys you thought were separate are really all connected around the base of the hills. Streams running through the valley join together more and more until they are one great river, flowing into the great oneness of the ocean.

35

Mudras and Mantras

As I continue to practice the mudras and mantras on Miao's DVD every day, both the eleven specific practices for healing and the additional practices that are part of Yoga of Joy, I feel more and more calm and centered and more and more joyful and loving. I begin to have the experience of being fully in the present moment, and I often experience being bathed in golden light. My body seems to be getting less and less solid; I often experience that there is only an outline of form when I am practicing, and the rest of me seems to be pure light energy. I love this feeling. I can hardly wait to begin my practices each day, and afterwards I linger longer and longer in meditation, just absorbing the pure light. I am actually having the *experience* of form dissolving into formlessness, and I know I can be an active participant in creating a new and healthy form.

What is happening here? What exactly is going on when I do the mudras and mantras? Reviewing my thoughts from the early Blue Pearl Groups, I remember that mudras are shapes formed by the ten fingers. We actually see them used casually everyday: we give thumbs up, flash the peace sign, shake hands on a deal. I know they are a kind of symbolic language, a way to communicate without words, but with a strong energetic message.

We also have our human mantras that we unconsciously repeat every day, adding to their power: "Right on!", or on a different day, "Life sucks."

I don't know so much about the ancient, more esoteric mudras and mantras, so I ask Miao. She tells me that ancient peoples didn't talk much. Their communication was primarily a language of vibration, communicated through mudras and mantras. Using pure vibration, a rich message could be delivered in a very simple way. She also says that ancient peoples were more familiar than we are with using this language to connect with divine energy. We all have that memory in our DNA, but unfortunately, in our modern world as we are less and less connected to our perfect essential nature, our Blue Pearl, we use this kind of language in a superficial way. Our mudras and mantras have devolved into mere gestures or phrases, often imbued with base intentions.

Guan Yin holds the Blue Pearl between her thumb and index finger, representing her ultimate connection to her perfect essential nature. In the Western world so few of us can hold our inner happiness that we often see people using these same two fingers to hold a marijuana joint. A friend of mine refers to this as the "smoking mudra."

"Oh, Jesus," used to be a serious calling out to the divine with a sincere heart; it has now become perverted into a universal expression of disgust or, as it is repeated in gyms and on athletic fields across the nation, an angry response to pain.

With the clarity that comes from observing a new culture, Miao says," 'Oh, shit,' and 'Fuck you,' are very popular mantras in the Western world." I'm realizing she is right, we hear these mantras across shopping malls, school parking lots and even places of business every day. I'm guilty of using them myself. I used to think this was all benign, and my '60s self bristled at the "uptightness" of those who objected. But as I think about our actual collective vibration I have to wonder. Miao says, "The Divine is saying, 'Oh, my children, I gave you the good mudra and mantra, but now you've changed it.'" And I have to wonder about the ultimate effect this change is having on our lives.

There is a long history to the use of mudra and mantra. Many ancient cultures used hand signs in art, dance, rituals, religious ceremonies, esoteric spiritual practices, and for healing. We see mudras in Egyptian hieroglyphics and early Christian art. They are also common in Hindu, Buddhist, Taoist and Jain tantric traditions.

Many of the mudras passed down from these ancient traditions work with specific pathways in both our physical and energetic bodies. In traditional Chinese medicine it is believed that there are channels called meridians along which energy flows throughout the "psychophysical" system. It is believed that disturbances in our physical and psychological states create blockages or imbalances in the flow of energy, or *qi,* throughout these meridians. Health is restored by reestablishing optimal flow and rebalancing *qi* throughout the system. The mudras facilitate this by activating acupressure points in the hands and engaging opposing poles in the body's electromagnetic field, adjusting imbalances in the body.

In China it is said, "The ten fingers connect with the heart," because three *yin* and three *yang* meridians come to the surface in each hand. They are believed to be connected to the five elements related to healing: metal, wood, fire, water and earth. The ten fingers are also thought to be intricately connected to one's mental intention. Western medicine emphasizes that the hands and fingers are well-supplied with peripheral nerves that directly connect to the central nervous system. So it makes sense that forming these hand positions can have a beneficial effect on the mental, emotional and physical systems.

But I sense there is something deeper going on when I experience all the golden light. The mudras I am practicing belong to the Vajrayana practice of "body tantra." Miao has told me that these sacred mudras originated as the spontaneous, natural expression of innate pristine awareness when sages and yogis, in deep states of meditation, achieved a state of "emptiness." These mudras arose out of the state of enlightenment.

Sacred mantras came into awareness in the same way. The source of words for the mantras is from Sanskrit, which is believed by some to be based on sound that comes from the divine. Miao says, "Both sacred mudra and mantra are manifestations with compassion of divine love."

The purpose of doing sacred mudra and mantra is not only to receive this energy, but also to ***be*** divine energy. It is a two way street. If we are in a state of emptiness, divine consciousness manifests as mudra and mantra. We can also reconnect to divine consciousness by forming the mudras and chanting the mantras. What makes the connection happen is belief and intention. Then the mudras and mantras can remove the troubled mind and promote healing on all levels.

But it is even more profound than this. I believe the importance of connecting to this divine source is that there is an actual vibration; it ripples outward, like the ripples in a pond when you throw in a pebble. There are certain people who radiate "good energy." We feel hopeful, positive and joyful around them. (I suspect the halos depicted around all the holy people in the Bible are a representation of this divine energy emanating from them). When we part company we often still feel that good feeling and we pass it along to others. Energy is moving, being spread person to person, sort of like a divine virus.

But even if we are alone, not in direct contact with another human being, I believe that when we connect with that divine energy, it goes rippling out into the universe anyway and has an effect. There is actually scientific theory to support this notion. In chaos theory from quantum physics there is a concept known as sensitive dependence on initial conditions. The idea is that, "small changes in the initial conditions of a dynamical system may produce large variations in the long term behavior of the system." You may have heard this referred to as the "butterfly effect": the idea that the flapping of a single butterfly's wings may insert one small change in the initial conditions which can have profound effects down the line.

Miao is offering, through her practices, a way to reconnect with the divine language and vibration of sacred mudra and mantra. Which mudras and mantras do you choose to strengthen every day?

36

Esoteric Healings

An email announcement from the Blue Pearl Group arrives in my in-box:

> At our next meeting Yuan Miao will be doing a special esoteric healing ceremony. Please join us.

The ceremony will be held in the evening on the same day as my next chemotherapy appointment. There is no ambivalence in me; I cannot miss this ceremony. Miao has never done something like this with us before and it is another of those "coincidences" that it will be happening at a critical point in my cancer treatment.

After the chemotherapy, I am feeling dazed and weak. While I use all of my energy to slouch against the car door, Gary drives with steely resolve the hour and a half from Palo Alto directly to Mill Valley for the meeting of the Blue Pearl Group.

There is an electric energy in the room. Miao's eyes are open and clear, radiating a quality of vast spaciousness. I sense she is deeply connected to another plane of existence, and I feel connected to a reality beyond the mind.

We all chant the Guan Shi Yin Pu Sa song, which is intended to call in all of the entities of love, compassion and healing, whoever those may be for each of us. Miao is doing her deep, mantric, vibratory chanting of primordial sounds, as her beautiful hands are forming amazing mudras, seamlessly flowing one into another.

She gives each of us a slip of paper on which we can write the names of up to three persons for whom we intend healing, and what the conditions are that need to be healed. I boldly include myself as one of my three. We then enter a meditative state during which Miao moves around the group, offering a healing to each person. Circling behind us, her helpers produce mystical sounds from Tibetan bells, bowls and gongs.

Seeming to sense individual need, Miao offers something unique to each person. To some she gazes into their eyes, to others she gently touches them at significant places, like the heart; to others she hits them seemingly quite hard on places like the shoulders or back.

I am in such a meditative trance by then, that what she does to me seems dreamlike. Most of it is gentle and loving, but then there is a more vigorous jolt that is the result of both physical contact and a guttural sound almost like a growl. I feel like the cancer is being both loved into transformation, and ordered to leave. Miao is both the loving mother and the stern, uncompromising father.

Telling us that in six days it will be the new moon, Miao instructs us to go outside at exactly 10:30 that night—the exact moment of the new moon. We are to sing the Blue Pearl song three times while burning a stick of incense. Then we are to carefully set fire to the pieces of paper with the names and the conditions to be healed, and bury them in the ground.

Upon returning home after the meeting, I vomit and vomit for the first time since beginning my chemotherapy treatment. I vomit until I have only dry heaves and then vomit some more. Gary holds me and says over and over, "That's good! The cancer is leaving your body."

Six days later, at exactly 10:30 p.m., Gary and I bundle up in our warmest ski jackets and scarves, and huddle outside by our lilac bush to be out of the wind. Holding our burning stick of incense, we sing as if our lives depend on it, and I believe that mine truly does. I stare at the pile of ashes in our hands before we bury them beneath our Buddha statue around which tiny white flowers continue to bloom year after year.

The next day, Gary hears that the Dalai Lama will be making a rare appearance in San Francisco, twelve days after we perform this ceremony. He does not hesitate to purchase our tickets.

Because the Dalai Lama appearance is so soon after the third chemotherapy, my white blood counts are low and I am in that period of time when I am vulnerable to all germs. It is questionable to go into a public auditorium filled with huge numbers of people and probably thousands of germs. Making the judgment call that the potential benefit outweighs the risk, I decide that no germ could survive in an auditorium filled with enlightened people in the presence of the Dalai Lama.

Clutching my wig, which threatens to blow off in the wind, feeling vulnerable and disoriented, I walk along the busy San Francisco street from parking lot to auditorium where colorful Tibetan prayer flags wave, and activists of all sorts are distributing flyers describing the plight of Tibet and asking for donations.

Entering the cavernous auditorium, we make a wrong turn and end up in the wrong tier of seats. The place is enormous, but we finally find the correct staircase, section, and are about to proceed to our row and seats when one of my contact lenses falls out of my eye. It seems like an impossible situation; there are hundreds of people passing, filling the aisles and looking for their seats. The lights are dim, the linoleum floor dark and speckled.

In that slow motion of dreams and accidents, a woman appears, asks what we are looking for, bends down, picks up the contact from under a seat, smiles and says, "Here it is," just like that. I believe that it is a sign that everything here is auspicious. For a brief moment we had lost our way and I had lost my vision, but both were easily restored to me.

When the Dalai Lama enters, the room is filled with palpable energy. I have the same sensation I had the night of Miao's healing ceremony when I looked into her eyes, of being connected to reality beyond the mind. This is the place described by the Romantic poets, a place of immortality and ultimate, transcendent reality. Unable to focus on what the Dalai Lama is actually saying, the healing for me is not through words or cognitive understanding, but from connecting to the pure, healing energy in the room.

As I predicted, I do not contract any illness or infection, and three days later I have my fourth chemotherapy, the last before my scheduled mid-treatment PET scan which will show how successful treatment has been so far.

37

Letting Go: How to Eliminate Sadness

Two days after my fourth chemotherapy, I wake up in the morning in my bed feeling cozy, no longer truly sleepy-tired, but not wanting to relinquish the warmth of my smooth yellow sheets pulled close around my shoulders. It is raining and cold outside, and I am still in that lingering, almost-dream state of just awakening.

I'm dreaming I am back in my childhood bedroom in our big, old wood frame house outside of our small town in South Dakota. It is winter and very cold and snowy outside. In my dream, I am cuddled under the blankets in my upstairs attic room where it is warm and comfortable. I hear the sounds of my mother in the kitchen downstairs, and I feel completely safe in the world. Wishing I could just stay in my bed feeling this way forever, I luxuriate in slow motion, savoring the feeling of not needing to hurry.

Shaking off the residue of this dream, still disoriented by a sense of the presence of my mother, I sit up in bed trying to reorient myself to present time. A year and a half has passed since her death. After her memorial service, I returned to California and went back to work. I was busy with a full time psychotherapy practice, parenting a fifteen-year-old son, and eventually caring in our home for my father who suddenly needed full time care from my sister and me. Five months after my sister began her turn caring for him, I was diagnosed with lymphoma. I realize I did not have time or space to do any grieving for my mother for many months.

It is only since the diagnosis of the lymphoma and the leave of absence from my practice that I have begun to experience waves of sadness about my mother when I meditate. I begin to see the image more and more frequently of her still lying there dead in the hospital bed, pink roses on her breast, and I am disturbed by it.

I have already returned to treatment with a clinical psychologist for hypnosis to explore the general question of whether there is anything subconscious which has either contributed to my developing lymphoma, or that is getting in the way of my recovering. As I get out of bed, I know I want to use the hypnosis to work with this image of my mother.

That evening, as I labor up the stairs to our Blue Pearl haven in the community center, I am still thinking about my mother lying dead in that hospital room. The repeated rounds of chemo have taken their toll, and it is more difficult to both find the energy to climb the stairs and to concentrate on anything anyone says to me. Floating in my "chemo brain" state in which I am truly cognitively compromised, I take in only fragments of what Yuan Miao is saying. The evening's topic is, "How to Eliminate Sadness," and I know my task is to hear the pearl that will help me with the loss of my mother.

"Attachment. Letting go," Miao is saying. There is the long, open, expansive pause. "Only by grounding one's heart in the impermanence of all things can we truly be free from meaningless afflictions caused by attachment." There it is: the pearl I need, glowing and beautiful with its simple wisdom.

Two days later, I remind my psychologist that one of the things happening with lymphoma is that the malignant lymphocytes have figured out how to be immortal. The normal lymphocytes should have a life cycle. The malignant ones hang on, refusing to die and this creates tumors. I think this may be related to my mother's death in some way. It is difficult to not wonder about the timing; my mother died and a year and a half later I was diagnosed with lymphoma.

We begin to work with the image of my mother, lying dead in the hospital bed. I realize immediately that I do not want to let her go. Somehow as long as I hold her there still embodied in the hospital bed, she is not really gone. My family's trust in hard work being able to control outcome is fully in play. I believe there must be something I can do, something that can prevent this loss.

I am holding my mother in some kind of suspended animation, unable to let her go, with some completely irrational, fully subconscious idea that as long as she is still there in that hospital bed and I hold onto her, she can be immortal in some way. The parallel with the lymphoma process is all too clear.

As I sit with the image and let the concepts of impermanence, letting go and transformation float through my hypnotized altered state, I begin to see the image of my mother breaking up into fragments. It reminds me of the way in late winter in the Midwest the thin ice, covering large holes in fields or on potholes in country gravel roads, begins to crack on the surface as the lower layers become liquid with the warming days. I can still see her image, but it is beginning to look more like fragments still fitted together like an intact jigsaw puzzle.

As I watch, the fragments begin to separate more and more into distinct pieces. The pieces begin to rise up, becoming more and more separate, and spread out. Then they break up into smaller and smaller pieces, continuing to float higher and higher. They are glowing and sparkling like some kind of fairy dust, and I know I am finally letting my mother go; I am letting her transform into pure energy and she is beautiful in this new state, free to once again be her shining, radiant self on a completely new plane of existence, where the old physical form is no longer necessary. She looks the way I feel when I do the sacred mudras and mantras.

It is a transformative lesson in letting go, because in a totally unexpected way I feel she is accessible to me again. I can feel her freedom and expansiveness and joyful spirit when I think of her.

For several weeks, when I think of the hospital bed I still see her there in her jigsaw form, but gradually, more and more, the form is less distinct and I see her more as the shining, rising fairy dust.

Now when I envision the hospital bed it is just an empty bed with new, clean white sheets folded neatly down at the top and tucked in tight under the mattress.

I don't know what happened to my malignant lymphocytes that day, or in the aftermath. My sense is that I took a big step toward letting them go. I have an image of them dying, and new, young, healthy lymphocytes coming and placing them in beautiful wooden coffins with white lilies on the covers. The coffins are taken to a huge funeral pyre, where periodically there is a wonderful ceremony honoring them for all they did to try to help my immune system and then all the coffins are burned. The heat and smoke rise up, spiraling into the sky where I know their energy joins with the energy of all transformed beings, including my mother.

I think it is no surprise that they placed my mother in a room on the maternity ward the day she died. Supposedly that was the only room available, but I have learned to trust the capricious ways of the universe more than to believe that. She was giving birth once again, this time a rebirth much like the process I am now going through myself.

She had a huge transformational task to go through, involving leaving the old form behind. I feel my own transformational task is to leave many old forms behind, including the one my mother shed that day.

I am just a couple of years behind her in being able to fully embrace her new form. I know I cannot release those malignant lymphocytes, which are refusing to let go in an ill-guided attempt at immortality, until I learn the lesson that embracing letting go and allowing transformation is our only hope for achieving something that may be like immortality.

PRACTICE

How to Release Sadness

Day 1

Meditate deeply on the impermanence of all things. Impermanence is the natural order of the universe. Miao says, "When a door closes, a window opens." Today, each time you think of a loss or an ending, try to imagine the window that has opened. When cancer and I closed the door on my psychotherapy practice, the window opened to write this book!

Day 2

Vajra Wind. This Vajra Wind exercise uses simple breathing and movement to help release sadness. It is helpful for the lungs, which according to Traditional Chinese Medicine can be negatively impacted by unresolved sadness. Stand with feet shoulder width apart, tall but relaxed, with arms at your sides. Inhale through your nose. Place your hands, palms facing up, fingertips at ears, at shoulder height and exhale, making the sound of "tsss" (like a snake), and press up to lift the sky. Eyes are wide to allow toxins to escape with the breath. Inhale as you ripple fingers like rain and move hands downward, palms facing ears. Repeat seven times.

Day 3

Mudra. Mood Elevating Mudra. If you did the first set of mudra exercises on page 66, you have already learned this mudra, but I will review the steps here. Cross the fingers of each hand as you would to indicate good luck (middle finger over index finger.) On each hand,

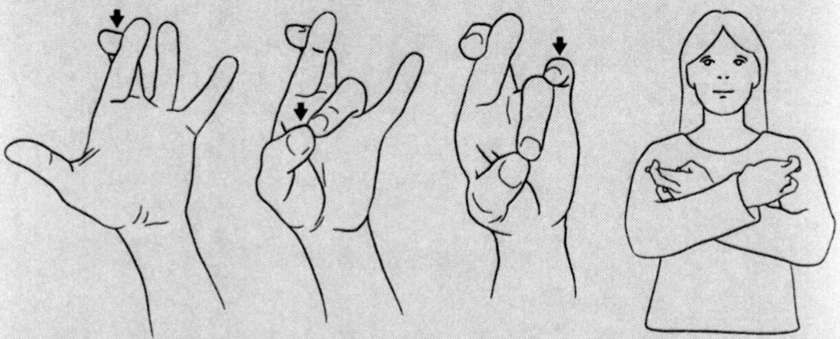

touch thumb nails to tips of ring fingers. On each hand, place the tip of little finger (pinky) on top of the knuckle of ring finger. Cross hands in front of your chest and relax your muscles. Practice forming and releasing mudra until you feel comfortable. Take a deep breath and relax your muscles. Close your eyes and focus on the mudra. Take time to feel its shape. Try to sense the actual vibration associated with the shape (if you can't sense this yet, just try to open to the possibility that there is such a vibration.) Then try to sense your own energetic vibration and align it with the vibration of the mudra.

Day 4

Mantra: Om Mani Padme Hum (The Precious Jewel Within the Lotus). Sit quietly. Close your eyes, relax your muscles and clear your mind. Visualize a blue pearl floating in a lovely lotus blossom. The lotus blossom rises through mud, unstained. The blue pearl is our perfect essential nature. Inhale through your nose using the visualization from The Breath of Light. (p. 65) As you exhale, chant **Om Mani Padme Hum** (Oh Mahnee Paid May Home) in a long, slow, sustained tone, while you imagine sound vibration and white light energy radiating outward and permeating every cell. Chant for at least five minutes.

Day 5

Color visualization. Sit quietly. Close your eyes, relax your muscles and clear your mind. Visualize the colors deep red, yellow, and light blue. Try to sense the vibration of each color. Try to align your energetic vibration to the frequency you sense from each color.

Day 6

Intention. Sit quietly and take the time to formulate a clear intention for this practice. Remember, intentions are most effective if they are positive (what you DO want) and in the present tense. The intention should be your own, but an example is, "I am releasing sadness and filling my heart with the healing energy of the blue pearl."

Day 7

Putting it all together

Repeat the Vajra Wind exercise for releasing sadness seven times.

Sit quietly. Close your eyes, relax your muscles and breathe naturally.

Form the Mood Elevating Mudra..

Focus on your intention.

Visualize the colors deep red, yellow and light blue.

Inhale using the pattern from The Breath of Light. As you exhale, chant Om Mani Padme Hum as you feel the sound vibration radiating outward from your center and permeating all of your cells.

Continue for at least five minutes, increasing the amount of time as you feel comfortable.

Finish your exercise by listening to **metal sounds**. Miao teaches these sounds are healing for the lungs and good for releasing sadness. (Listen to Tibetan singing bowls, sound a Tibetan tingsha, play a metal flute, ring metal bells or gongs.)

38

Lashed to the Mast

From: **Susan Sattler**
Date: **May 16, 2007 10:38 PM**
Subject: **Susan Tries to Enjoy Smaller, Moonlit Storm from Top of Mast**

Hi Everyone,

Well, metaphorically speaking I did as I intended and lashed myself to the mast last May 2nd (Chemo #4). My intention, as you recall, was to attempt to follow John Muir's example of lashing himself to a tall tree in the Sierras during a storm so he could enjoy the ride. My friend Jeanne had emailed me ahead of time that I should remember that the magical full moon would be riding with me on May 2nd. I looked on my calendar, and sure enough there was to be a full moon on the night of Chemo #4.

So, here's the image for that night. I have crawled to the highest point I can reach on the rigging of my ship. I have lashed myself securely to the mast and wish I could let my hair blow in the wind, but since I am now bald, I have to enjoy the breezes on my bare scalp. The ship is rolling over medium sized waves and I am actually fine with it so far. I look up to check on my moon companion and sure enough there it is, reassuring me with its predictable monthly fullness.

The lines from a long-ago declamation contest which I won in junior high float through my mind, "The moon was a ghostly galleon, tossed upon cloudy seas ..." And I wait as we sail through the night. Sure enough, the winds pick up, the waves grow larger, and the boat begins to be tossed about. (In real life, blunt terms, I start vomiting again. I have a splitting headache and wish I could crawl out of my body. Metaphor is so much nicer, don't you think?)

I feel the fear begin to take its grasp around the back of my neck. Is this storm going to get worse? How long will it last? What if the ship breaks apart and we all drown? What if I'm permanently damaged in the end? What if, what if, what if ...?

So I take myself in hand and try to remember my intention to stay present with the ride. As I'm buffeted around on the mast of my ship, I try to trust that this is just a storm, it will pass and there will be calm seas, probably even beautiful days ahead. So this is the concept of impermanence. I can trust that, and I find it frees me to be more interested in the experience at hand. Although I'm uncomfortable, it's really only a bumpy ride. If I'm not scared, I find I'm less uncomfortable. I can look up and even enjoy watching the moon taking its own bumpy ride.

By morning I am no longer vomiting, so I am feeling much better. My wonderful neighbor Sheila gives me a Jin Shin treatment (which uses acupressure to harmonize body, mind and spirit), balancing all of my energy and making sure it is flowing in the right direction. While I certainly did not feel normal or great for several days, I did not feel like the mother ship was going down.

By day eight, I was mostly experiencing weakness and fatigue, and by Mother's Day, I was able to go on a nice long hike with Gary and Toby. I don't know that I can claim to have really found a thrill in the ride like John Muir, but I know I made progress in surrendering to the experience. Perhaps my attitude helped shorten the storm. I kept thinking of the A.A. twelve step program phrase, "What you resist persists." I was trying my best to not resist the ride.

So tomorrow, Thursday May 17th, is a milestone event. I will go to Stanford for a PET scan, which will be the first time since I began treatment that my doctors will actually be able to look at what is happening with my malignant lymph nodes. The technique is pretty interesting. They inject a glucose-like substance that has been paired with a radioactive isotope into my vein. The cells with the highest rate of metabolism suck up the glucose-like substance and inadvertently, the radioactive isotope. The fastest growing cells with the highest rate of metabolism are the cancer cells, of course, so those areas light up on the radiologist's screen like a Christmas tree. They can compare this scan with the one I did at the beginning of treatment to see how we are doing.

The goal is to get me into complete remission. If we can achieve that, they do two more treatments because, although the scan may not be showing any malignant activity, there may still be microscopic aberrant cells migrating around, unable to be detected by current diagnostic techniques. If I do not go into complete remission, we persevere with ongoing treatments that may change if we do not make progress. I will not know the results of the scan until I see my doctor again.

So, obviously what I am hoping for, and holding in my intention, is that this scan will show I am in complete remission now. I appreciate all your good thoughts and prayers to this end. If you like visualization you could visualize any last remaining malignant lymphocytes dissolving into an energy form which can transform and move on to another plane of existence.

As always, thank you all for being the wonderful people that you are. A true healer and former teacher of mine, Angeles Arrien, stressed the necessity of "walking the spiritual path with practical feet." A major component of that is "to show up." I am awed at all the ways you have, and continue to "show up" for me. There are now many beautiful, spiritual paths leading to our door, well worn by your steadfast, practical feet.

Love and gratitude,

Susan

39

How to Achieve Harmony and Balance

Somehow winter has transitioned through spring and into summer. As I cross the parking lot of the community center everyone is in tank tops, halter tops, flip flops and shorts. As two trails of perspiration race each other to my chin, I begin to notice how incredibly hot wigs are in warm weather.

Arriving a little late, I make a bee-line for the Blue Pearl room where even Miao is wearing a short sleeved red silk top, her long black hair held up in a knot by a wooden Chinese stick. This will be the last Blue Pearl group that she will lead for many weeks because she is leaving to travel to China and Malaysia. Impermanence. There are easily 25 people in the room, none of whom wants to miss this last opportunity to be in her presence before she leaves.

Blue Pearl, Blue Pearl, love and compassion,
most precious jewel.
Blue Pearl, Blue Pearl, the most auspicious,
most precious jewel.
Blue Pearl, Blue Pearl, atop of the lotus,
most precious jewel.

Blue, Pearl, Blue Pearl, magical power,
most precious jewel.
Blue Pearl, Blue Pearl, from emptiness,
most precious jewel.
Blue Pearl, Blue Pearl, from the mantra,
most precious jewel."

Using a guitar-like pick, Miao plucks perfect notes on her Chinese harp as we sing.

"Surrender," Miao fixes us with her centered, oceanic gaze. Timeless time passes. "Surrender." More time. "Courage, trust, you have to have faith."

I'm trying to stay connected to her spacious mind, but I find myself remembering something another woman in the group said a few weeks previously, "Gratitude is the mother of faith." My heart is filled with gratitude for all the blessings I have received, and I realize that it is the resulting faith that has inspired me to stick to my practice of mudras, mantras, Yoga of Joy, meditation and walking in nature every day through my cancer treatment. Even though it has required a two and a half to three hour commitment each day, and there were certainly times when my physical body was compromised (when I felt tired, or sick, or when I was throwing up), I haven't missed a day yet. I have meditated on grasping, attachment, impermanence, greed and illusion, and tried to address these issues in my life with faith that the universal wisdom Miao has been teaching will bring me peace, harmony and balance. I trust that it is these qualities that will return me to optimal health.

I hear Miao's voice through my thoughts, "When you sow compassion, peace of mind is reaped in like measure. When we express wisdom, the return is tranquility." There is a vast, spacious silence. "Remember the Chinese characters for busy are Heart/Death."

I think about how busy and frenetic my life used to be. I think about how now one day unfolds into the next with a rhythm of its own, like being carried on gentle waves, washing in, washing out. When I surrender to whatever may come to me from the upcoming PET scan and trust that I will find a way to have "That's good!" apply no matter what the result, I feel peace, harmony and balance. Over the past weeks as I've committed to the practices, I have entered a state of no fear; I have felt I could accept anything. Now that is put to the test; I have to say goodbye to my beautiful teacher.

With tears streaming down my face, I say my goodbyes to Miao. Impermanence. Just as she appeared when my client took his life, guided me through that transformation and then was gone, now she has apparently taken me as far as necessary through these challenging times, giving me the tools I need to not only survive, but to shed yet another skin.

Arriving home, I am thinking about wisdom. It is such a common word; one of those words I use without thinking about its complexity. Miao has just said, "When we apply wisdom, the result is tranquility." Why is that? Interested in understanding more about wisdom, I do some research, and this is what I find:

"Wisdom is a deep understanding of people, things, events or situations, resulting in the ability to choose or act to consistently produce the optimum results with a minimum of time and energy. Wisdom often requires control of one's emotional reactions (the 'passions') so that one's principles, reason and knowledge prevail to determine one's actions."

Producing optimal results with a minimum of time and energy would definitely contribute to tranquility. Miao emphasizes overcoming ego and offering love and compassion. When our focus is not primarily on ourselves and on our own needs, we have a much better chance of developing a deep understanding of people, things, events or situations. I find that when my mind is clear and quiet it is much easier to control my emotional reactions and to easily see what action is needed.

I realize that all of the practices Miao has generously shared with us:

the mudras, mantras, Yoga of Joy, and breathing and meditation exercises, are the tools to help quiet our "monkey mind," so that we may develop wisdom and its gift of tranquility.

I'm remembering that as we were leaving the Blue Pearl Group, Miao posed a parting question to all of us 'pearls,' "How deep in your heart is the Blue Pearl?" I reach deep into my heart for the compassion and wisdom that will give me the needed peace of mind and tranquility to continue on my journey.

PRACTICE

How to Achieve Harmony and Balance

Day 1

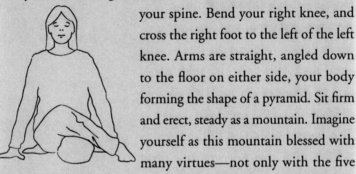

Sitting on the floor, bend your left leg underneath you, and press your left heel against the root chakra located at the base of your spine. Bend your right knee, and cross the right foot to the left of the left knee. Arms are straight, angled down to the floor on either side, your body forming the shape of a pyramid. Sit firm and erect, steady as a mountain. Imagine yourself as this mountain blessed with many virtues—not only with the five elements (metal, wood, water, fire and earth) in harmonious balance, but also possessing wisdom and compassion. Hold this position until you fully absorb the visualization. Then bend your right leg underneath you, and press your right heel against your root chakra. Cross your left leg over the right and repeat the visualization.

Day 2

Vajra Wind. This Vajra Wind exercise uses simple breathing and movement to help balance and harmonize your entire system. It is helpful for the endocrine and hormonal systems, which according to Traditional Chinese Medicine can be negatively impacted by imbalance. This exercise can be done standing up or sitting down. The position is slightly different for men than for women. For

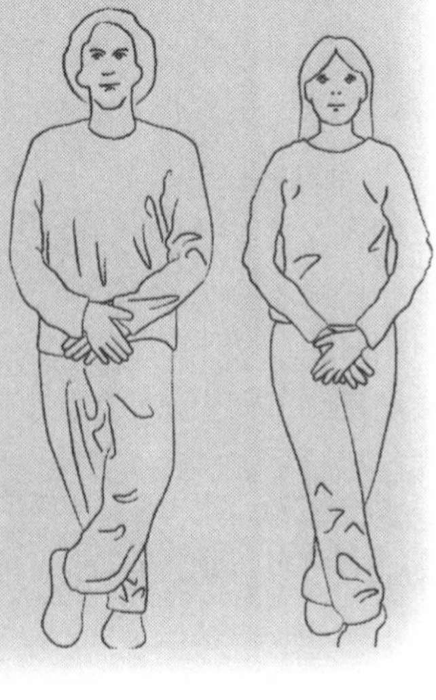

men, left leg is crossed over right and left hand covers the navel, palm down. Right hand is placed over the left. For women, right leg is crossed over left, and right hand covers the navel, palm down. Left hand is placed over the right. Inhale through your nose. As you exhale make the Chinese sound of "Xi" (Tsshh) by sending air over the top of a flat tongue. Repeat seven times.

Day 3

Mudra: Harmonizing and Balancing Mudra. This mudra also supports the endocrine and hormonal systems. Form two circles with your fingers by touching nails of index fingers to tips of thumbs. Touch these two circles so they look like eyeglasses in front of you. Then extend middle and ring fingers and touch tips of right to tips of left. Spreading the little fingers as far away as possible, touch their tips, and stretch the whole configuration. Place the mudra at the heart center. Men leave fingers pointing up, women turn mudra upside down.

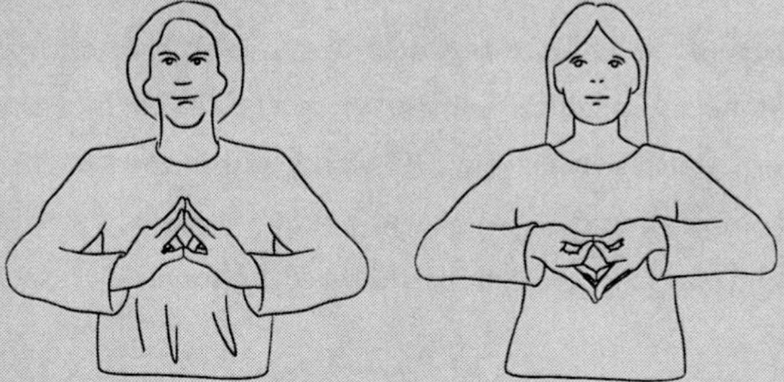

Practice forming and releasing this mudra until you feel comfortable. Then form the mudra, take a deep breath, and relax your muscles. Close your eyes and focus on the mudra. Take time to feel its shape. Try to sense the actual vibration associated with the shape (if you can't sense this yet, just try to open to the possibility that there is such a vibration.) Then try to sense your own energetic vibration and align it with the vibration of the mudra.

Day 4

Mantra: Damo Da Hum Hum. Sit quietly with hands resting comfortably on your thighs. Close your eyes, relax your muscles and clear your mind. Inhale through your nose as you do the visualization of The Breath of Light. (p. 65) Choose a single tone and as you exhale chant **Damo Da Hum Hum** (Dahmo Dah Home Home) while you imagine white light energy and sound vibration radiating outward and permeating every cell. Chant for at least five minutes.

Day 5

Color visualization. Sit quietly. Close your eyes, relax your muscles and clear your mind. Visualize the colors purple, light blue and grass green. Try to sense the vibration of each color. Light is electromagnetic energy and each color has a different wave length, giving it a particular frequency. Try to align your energetic vibration to that of each color.

Day 6

Intention. Sit quietly and take the time to formulate a clear intention for this practice. Remember, intentions are most effective if they are positive (what you DO want) and in the present tense. The intention should be your own, but an example is, "My energy is balanced and I am living in harmony with the world around me."

Day 7

Putting it all together

Repeat the Vajra Wind exercise to help balance and harmonize your system seven times

Sit quietly. Close your eyes, relax your muscles and breathe naturally.

Form the Harmonizing and Balancing Mudra

Repeat your intention slowly three times.

Visualize the colors purple, light blue and grass green.

While still holding the mudra, inhale using the visualization from The Breath of Light. As you exhale, chant Damo Da Hum Hum as you imagine sound vibration radiating outward from your center and permeating all of your cells. Continue for at least five minutes, increasing the amount of time as you feel comfortable.

Finish your exercise by listening to **classical music**, which integrates all of the sounds of water, wood, air, metal and earth.

If you are serious about developing a practice, I suggest making a commitment to doing this exercise for 40 days.

40

Scans and More Scans

From: **Susan Sattler**
Date: **May 21, 2007 11:32 PM**
Subject: **Susan's Lymph Nodes**

Hi Everyone,

I appreciate all your warm thoughts and inquiries about my PET scan. I think I have great news, but as always in this journey, it's a little more complicated than I thought. My doctor tells me that the PET scan "did not show any activity."

I say, "So then I am in complete remission?" She then explains that they do not use that term until treatment is completed. Apparently the PET is one diagnostic tool and it is now showing I have a "complete response."

Therefore, the treatment plan will continue to be six sessions of Chemo, of which I have completed 4, and six of Rituxan of which I have completed 3. At the end of treatment they will use another diagnostic test, a high contrast CT scan through which they actually measure my lymph nodes, which is something the PET does not do. Apparently they are unwilling to proclaim anything as sweeping as complete remission until treatment is complete and the final CT has been evaluated.

However, I think we can all celebrate because I think the PET is the latest, state of the art diagnostic tool, and if it does not show any unusual metabolic activity now (and I assure you there was plenty of it on my initial PET), I feel pretty confident that after two more rounds of Chemo and three more treatments of the wonder drug Rituxan, I can't imagine them suddenly finding something unexpected.

But my belief is that what the PET seems to indicate is true. I believe I have had a complete response to treatment and my treatment has been so much more than the Western drugs (though I do not in any way denigrate their contribution).

A huge part of my treatment has been being held in the love and caring of all of you amazing people. I have honestly been bathed in the radiant, golden light of love all spring. How could any misguided, malignant cell resist that kind of healing? I honestly do not know how to communicate the full depth of my gratitude, but I thank you and I know I am blessed to be cared about by each of you.

So, back on a practical plane, my white blood cell counts were too low today for me to have treatment, so they are now giving me three days of Neupogen shots to stimulate my bone marrow stem cells to produce white blood cells more quickly. The hope is that they can give me the Rituxan next Monday and Chemo #5 the following Wednesday. If we can stay on schedule I will have one more Chemo, and two final Rituxans. Hopefully that will be it and we can have a PARTY!!!!

My plan would be in August when you are all back from your fabulous summer vacations, like the weekend after school starts ... but perhaps I'm getting ahead of myself. I'll keep you posted!

Much love,

Susan

41

Dazed in the Doldrums

From: **Susan Sattler**
Date: **July 5, 2007, 10:34 PM**
Subject: **Susan Ends Up on Raft Caught in the "Doldrums"**

Hi everyone,

Many thanks for all of your inquiries about what has happened to me. I know there has been a big gap in my communication. I think I left you with the encouraging results of the PET scan done last May. At that time they also discovered that my white blood counts were too low to do Chemo #5. I was given a series of shots of a growth-stimulating hormone in the hopes it would encourage my stem cells in the bone marrow to pump out some white blood cells more quickly. Because I had been vomiting after previous treatments, they added another anti-emetic to my treatment regimen. Now pumped up like the athlete on steroids (and, in fact, actually on steroids since prednisone is one of my Chemo drugs) I was able to do Chemo #5.

I have no idea if what then happened was the cumulative result of all the treatment, or if the new drugs put their own spin on things, but I entered into about five weeks during which I wandered about in a fog.

Let us return to the ship metaphor. I somehow find myself off my ship on a small raft. I feel disoriented, not sure exactly how I got here. The sun is beating down, I'm trying to do the things necessary to survive, but I'm having trouble thinking and focusing.

I really only want to lie on the raft, but I have a vague knowledge that there are things I should be doing. I actually go through the motions of doing some of them, but it all seems dreamlike as one day flows into another and my sense of linear time and thought unravel. I ultimately just let go of the last vestige of attempted control, and hope the currents will continue to carry my raft to my intended destination.

Unfortunately, my raft gets caught in the doldrums, the area around the equator, known and feared by sailors because of its calms, squalls and light shifting winds. I don't seem to be making progress; I have the vague image of trudging through mud.

I really can't tell you what happened during this time. The day after Chemo #5 I had a big-boy version shot of the growth stimulating hormone to ensure my blood counts would not drop again. Days came and went and another Chemo happened on June 20th, followed by another big-boy shot. The raft just kept circling in the doldrums. I felt tired, and dazed, like I was going through the motions on drugs, and it occurs to me now as I'm coming out of all this, that, of course I WAS on drugs!!

Today is day fifteen after Chemo #6 and I am feeling somewhat normal, not dazed as if living life on drugs. I have two treatments to go at Stanford. They, too, are infusions through an IV but of only one drug, Rituxan, which is not so hard on the body.

We then wait two months and do the final CT scan so they can see what is going on with my lymph nodes when I am not in "active treatment". They want to be sure the result is not because the cancer is being temporarily suppressed by the treatment.

So, one would think that I would be feeling quite overjoyed that the end for now may be in sight, but paradoxically I have been quite teary and emotional. My best assessment is that I have mobilized my most functional self these past few months to be sure I took the best care of myself in all ways to optimize my chances of recovery. I certainly couldn't afford to decompensate and be an emotional mess.

It is only now as I may reach a safe haven of sorts that I can allow myself the luxury of feeling the full array of my feelings about the journey. I also think that this last month broke down whatever last barriers and defenses I had keeping the emotions at bay, sort of my personal EST experience.

So, about the PARTY!! I think I will wait until after the CT scan in September so our success won't be qualified. I can't tell you how fitting I think it is that this is the 40th anniversary of The Summer of Love in San Francisco!! You have all extended so much love to us during this journey; I want you all to come to the party so I can thank you and celebrate that love is still so alive in so many hearts! We will make it a "happening," more later, but trust me I will make it worthy of all of you and the anniversary of that great Summer of Love.

I hope you are all well. As always, thank you for continuing to be with us in so many ways on this challenging journey.

Much love and gratitude,

Susan

42

Arriving Back on Shore

From: **Susan Sattler**
Date: **August 28, 2007, 9:45 PM**
Subject: **Susan Thank You Party/Happening/Celebration of Love in Sonoma County**

Hi Everyone,

Well, the kids are back in school, the leaves are sounding crisper, most of you have gone on and returned from your summer vacations, and in the midst of it all my little raft washed me up on shore. It's a strange thing to have been away on a journey that was so intense that it required every ounce of my energy and attention, and to return to find life churning on in its usual way as if nothing has happened. I definitely feel like the seafarer, trying to figure out where I am, who I am, and where I fit into the grand scheme of things when I feel so changed by my experiences.

When I arrived back on shore after my final treatments, I was swept up in activity with loved ones greeting me at the shore, helping me from my raft and whisking me off on celebrations and reunions.

Gary, Toby and I spent four incredible days on a spectacular mountain lake in the Sierras. We had a terrific granite rock for jumping into the lake, spectacular fires, and the stars were awesome every night. It was there that I could begin to really embrace a mantra my psychologist suggested during hypnosis at our last session, "I survived! I am alive!"

The magnitude of that reality hit me full force in the mountains. The reality that there could have been, and still could be, a different outcome hit me with just as much force.

As Yuan Miao would say, "That's good!"

I get to be alive and I get to remember what it's like to see the world through newborn eyes. I get to embrace the Yin/Yang of fully, deeply loving this life and reality, and knowing at exactly the same moment that it is impermanent and one day I will let it go.

For now, I feel like I have been granted a rebirth. I've learned a great deal over the past eight months about letting go. I've let go of what now seem like small things, like my hair. I've let go of some major things, like my psychotherapy practice. I've begun walking down the path of learning to let go of fear, fear of the future, and of trying to control outcome. I know it is impossible to transform without discomfort and letting go of old, worn out identities and forms.

I feel like the new-born baby, vulnerable and recently delivered into an unfamiliar world, squinting at the bright lights. The old, familiar womb is gone. I feel like some capricious child picked up my colorful puzzle with all the pieces in place showing my former life, and dumped it all on the floor. I'm sure I'll find and decide to keep a few of the old pieces, but I am equally sure some are now gone, hurtling into the past forever.

As most of you know, I'm awaiting a CT scan to be done on September 10th with a follow-up appointment with my doctor on September 19th, at which time she will be able to tell me her assessment of how well the treatment has worked so far. She will certainly tell me if she recommends more treatment at this point in time, if something is there but we "watch and wait," or maybe she will even determine that I am now in complete remission.

At any rate, I am going with the belief that all will be good news and whatever the result, I want to thank you all for everything you've done, so it is time to have our party!!!

Bring your love beads, peace symbols, earth balls, and tie dyes! Also bring your kids of all ages. But most importantly, bring your love!!

Love and gratitude, as always,

Susan

43

Final Results

CALL IT TAO

Something mysteriously formed,
born before heaven and earth.

In the silence and the void,
standing alone and unchanging,
ever present and in motion.

Perhaps it is the mother
of ten thousand things.

I do not know its name.

Call it Tao.

—*Tao Te Ching*

On September 19, exactly nine months to the day from the first symptoms that had alerted me that there was something amiss in my body, Gary and I sit on hard plastic chairs waiting for the doctor who will give us the final report from the CT scan done last week. Metaphorically, we are anxiously waiting for the arrival of the new baby, nine months in the making. We have exhausted every possible avenue to insure health.

This baby has been lovingly cared for by doctors, friends, family members, spiritual masters and healers of all sorts. But will there be five fingers and five toes? Or in this case, will there be beautiful strands of healthy lymph glands with no nodes larger than one centimeter?

There is nothing cozy or pink or blue about this room where we wait. Everything here is sterile and neutral. A black blood pressure cuff hangs on the wall. White paper crackles on the black and chrome examining table, which is a perfect match for the stainless steel sink embedded in a black counter. I stare anxiously at the floor, a beige linoleum. There are no windows. The only access to the outside world is through a computer waiting to hungrily devour the comments I will give to the nurse practitioner before I see the doctor.

I am remembering being in labor with my son and how slowly it progressed: mine was the fifty hour labor, evidence of how long it could take a 41-year-old mother to let go. As I am reviewing that memory, I realize my personal rebirth that is now underway is about much more than my lymph nodes. Birthing my new way of being in the world is still in progress. I am passing milestones, making progress, but the journey of letting go and re-formation as a regular practice in real life is complex, complicated and will undoubtedly be lengthy.

I am remembering my son's anxious query when we told him I had cancer, "Are we going to be poor?"

And suddenly there is my doctor with the beautiful name, smiling at me and saying, "Your scan looks good. You continue to have a complete response. We'll now see you once every three months and you will have a CT scan every six months."

So just like that, there is the baby with all ten fingers and all ten toes, but still so vulnerable that it needs to be seen by a doctor on a regular basis. I expected to feel ecstatic, elated, overjoyed. I do feel great relief, gratitude and joy, but the truth is that from the Western medical perspective, there could still be undetectable "mother cells of cancer" which might be flying under the radar, rampantly spawning cancer cell babies. The clinical studies nurse admits, "We can't really breathe easy for at least two years."

So what do Gary and I do? We do what custom and tradition in the Western world dictate: we go out for lunch. We soak up the Stanford sunshine and smile at each other a lot. It is another of those moments between chapters, the tilt of the pinball machine. For now the Chemo game is over, but the new game has not yet begun. I decide to try to relax into the space.

44

The Summer of Love

Three days later Yuan Miao performs her First Annual World Music Concert for Universal Healing at the Marin County Civic Center. She floats in transcendent space, wearing a traditional white silk Chinese robe with long, fluid sleeves flowing around her.

The notes of "Guan Shi Yin Pu Sa" seem to emanate directly from her heart as she plucks the strings of her Guzheng harp, and I sense all the entities of love, compassion and healing surrounding us, celebrating life. Losing myself in the vibration of her deep mantric singing, I am back where I began my journey with her three years earlier. Since the night of that first meeting when I had the vision of the huge snake, slithering in the background, lulled by her primordial sounds, I have shed several skins myself, and I feel as raw, unprotected and vulnerable as snakes are said to feel after their transformation.

A few days later I am in our pasture laughing, as my beautiful, loving friends who brought food throughout my treatment, chauffeured me to appointments, accompanied me on walks, and lent support in ways too numerous to describe, come piling out of their cars. Dressed in their best tie dyes and love beads, they are ready to create the 40th Anniversary of the Summer of Love Happening on our property, the culmination and crescendo of the love and energy that has been building all winter, spring and summer.

I settle my back against an unoccupied hay bail and stretch my legs out in the Sonoma County late September sunshine as "Dead Walrus" (a band composed of Toby's friends) jump nimbly onto the stage, lovingly built by my husband and son over the past few days. Covered with scraps of old carpet with a wildly tie-dyed sheet forming the backdrop, it's a perfect tribute to The Summer of Love.

As their final metallic sounds fade beyond the horizon, Toby sits down at the keyboard, nods to his longtime music teacher on lead guitar and to the electric fiddle player, waits for the cue from the drummer, and sings:

Love is but the song I'm singing,
fear's the way we die.

You can make the mountains ring
or make the angels sigh.

Know that love is on the wing,
though you may not know why.

Come on people now,
smile on your brother.

Everybody get together.
Try to love one another right now.

It's the mantra for the day: everyone catches the feeling. More than a few tears are rolling down cheeks, and even Jesse Colin Young himself would have been moved.

Later as those words, "Fear's the way we die," echo in my mind, I dust off my own guitar and brave my stage fright. Looking fearlessly into the eyes of friends and family, I think of Bob Dylan and Joan Baez as I sing a song Miao sang at her concert:

May you build a ladder to the stars,
And climb on every rung.
May you stay forever young.

May your hands always be busy
May your feet always be swift
May you have a strong foundation
When the winds of changes shift

May your heart always be joyful
May your song always be sung
May you stay forever young.

Microphone still in hand, I try to express how happy I am to be given a new lease on life.

"Thank you all for coming. I just want to try to express my thanks to all of you in this community for all you did for us over the last many months. Look to your right, look to your left, and you will see someone who did amazing things for us with incredible love.

"So, I was thinking about the fact that this is the 40th anniversary of the Summer of Love, and remembering that back then there were all kinds of things that needed healing. I think the people coming together for the Summer of Love were trying to affirm the power of love to heal. There was the Vietnam War, there were civil rights issues, there were many, many problems, as we all know.

"And then I was thinking about how we now have another war, we have racism in other forms, we have problems right now today, but what I wanted to affirm, with you all coming together today, is life.

"It's a gorgeous day, I'm alive, you're alive, the people you love are here with you. What you've done for us—it's not just about me, it's about the power of love. I believe you all helped heal me, and if you can heal me we can heal amazing things in the world. Thank you from the bottom of my heart and I think you are all incredible people."

That evening as we all dance beneath the redwood trees, I feel like the richest person on earth. Here is the glimmering, first hint of the paradoxical answer to my son's question, "Are we going to be poor?"

The day after the party, I wander around in our yard, absently picking up stray purple napkins, a broken strand of love beads, half empty soda cans, a forgotten tie-dyed shirt. I have that slightly melancholic feeling of the party being over and it being time to get back to work.

But what exactly is my work going to be? I seem to have done a pretty good job of letting go of the old forms, but now that my active treatment is over, it is time for some reformation. Having dismantled my old life, I am faced with having to construct a new one. I am already haunted by the old mantra, "You'd better keep your nose to the grindstone."

But cancer and I have now radically changed my life. I don't have so much time, not to mention desire, for the old grindstone anymore. I have discovered I like the golden light and joyful vibration a lot more. My daily practice has become the centerpiece of my life: it really is the main course, not dessert. It was easy to justify this when I was trying to survive cancer, but now that I am in remission I know there will be other expectations of me. "Life is real and life is earnest."

Will I be able to stay in "No Fear" and design a radically new life?

After I had achieved a "complete response," we had a party of thanks to all those who helped in my healing.

45

Lessons from My Father

As I am struggling to learn to live with more surrender and trust, less control and fear, my father shows me the way. One evening just before Thanksgiving the phone rings and it is my sister calling from Massachusetts. Our 93-year-old father has been living with her in a suburb of Boston while I was doing chemotherapy.

"Susan," Ann begins. I know something is wrong. She rarely uses that form of my name. Usually I am still Sue to her. "Dad is in the hospital. He has developed serious pneumonia. The antibiotics are not working well yet, and he is really sick. Yes, I would say critically ill." A doctor, she does not use that term frivolously.

I am on an airplane by the next morning and at his bedside by that evening. I hold his burning hand and scrutinize his white face. Eyes are closed; an oxygen mask hides his mouth. He is gravely ill. Instinctively, I form the nerve health supporting mudra that always seems to calm me, and I visualize the healing energy of the Blue Pearl within my father.

It is touch and go for four days. I cling to the touchstone of my practices, doing my mudras and mantras and Yoga of Joy in the tiny attic bedroom of my sister's house, wanting to calm myself and call on the

Blue Pearl energy to help me stay connected to love and compassion. Still fearing judgment and knowing my family members do not have an experiential understanding of what I am doing, I try to chant softly so as not to appear too weird. My sister is supposed to be on a plane to India with her husband who is scheduled to speak at medical schools there; they forego their departure and we wait, pacing halls of the hospital, trying to make small talk with each other.

At night, I can't sleep. One night, as I lie awake, I'm remembering being back in South Dakota as a child. My mother, father, sister and I are in a tiny house trailer that smells of old bacon grease, visiting with an overweight, obviously unhealthy man. We are making our annual Christmas visit to Mr. Packer, a patient of my father's who is a "shut in." I'm only about six years old, but I get the idea that this man is too sick to go out, has no family to care for him, and that we are trying to bring some Christmas joy to him while my dad checks on his health. I watch as my dad gently lifts one of Mr. Packer's feet—somehow he seems to make it float effortlessly in his sensitive hands—and carefully removes the shoe and sock. A swollen, angry red mess reveals itself. I am horrified and afraid. But my dad is using a voice I've heard so often when I've hurt myself and I am scared—kind, not too serious, reassuring, confident.

"Well, old top, the ankle is acting up a bit today, isn't it? Let's see, we're going to have to get the old rascal to quiet down." (The old rascal? I'm in awe that my dad can use that description for this flaming mess.) I see Mr. Packer visibly relax.

"So, you don't think it's so bad, Doc? I'll be OK?" His relief is palpable. Now, as an adult, I realize that a critical part of his healing began right then as he experienced my father's compassion and felt trust and hope. My dad had the gift of ministering not only to the body, but also to mind and spirit.

I'm hoping the staff at the hospital can offer him the same kind of care that he spent a lifetime offering to others.

On the fourth day, he has responded well enough to the antibiotics that the hospital determines that although he is weak and will take a long time to recover, my father can be moved to a skilled-nursing rehabilitation center. My sister and I scout out the best we can find on short notice with an available bed. We stand in the hospital parking lot, shivering under grey East Coast November skies, and watch four orderlies push a gurney, holding the blanket-swathed form that is my father, to an ambulance. His eyes are closed; he doesn't move. I can't tell if he is asleep or if he is unconscious.

The ambulance crawls out of the parking lot, headed for the care facility. As I watch the tail lights disappear into the dark, I am that little South Dakota child watching her doctor father, hoping to save someone's life, disappear down a dark rural highway.

The next day, my sister, her family, and I are sitting around her dining room table, picking at our Thanksgiving turkey.

I raise my glass in a tentative toast, hoping to buoy the spirits of my niece and nephew. "I'm grateful for dad's progress." But my sister and I lock eyes, knowing there is a long road of recovery ahead of him.

"I think he is stable enough for Allan and I to leave on our trip," she says quietly after dinner. "A cab will pick us up at 4:00 a.m."

The following morning, she and her husband are on a plane to India, and I embark on a journey with my father to explore the realms of courage, faith, trust and surrender.

46

Sisters of Charity

I'm sitting in my father's room at the Sisters of Charity Residence. I've now spent nearly two weeks drifting with him in that timeless realm created by hospital stays and long old-age passages from this plane of existence to the next. He will eventually weather this storm just as I weathered mine, but also like me, he's danced closer to the other side and lingered there looking around, taking a longer look this time. I've been dancing with him, floating with angels on updrafts of love, meditation, memory and grace.

The Elizabeth Seton Sisters of Charity Residence is named in honor of Saint Elizabeth Ann Bayley Seton, the Foundress of the Sisters of Charity. She was a wife, a mother, and ultimately a devotee of the church. She began Catholic Education in the United States in the mid 1800s. She was the first American born woman to be canonized by the Roman Catholic Church.

The "mother house" of this order is located in Halifax, Nova Scotia. Here at Elizabeth Seton in Massachusetts there are 84 skilled nursing beds, and 94 residence beds for retired nuns who range in age from 80 to 103. There is a beautiful chapel and elderly nuns are praying, chanting and meditating throughout the day and night. I can feel the transcendent energy throughout the building, an energy of peace and tranquility. This is where the hospital located an available rehabilitation bed for my dad, but I believe it is divine intervention that we are here as opposed to some other generic nursing home. Here, as we both are healing, my father and I are reconnected to our shared Christian lineage.

My sister is still away on her trip to India, the heart of where spiritual seekers have gone for centuries to find spiritual connection. I would have liked to go too, but I know she will have many months ahead of her taking care of my dad, and this gives her a bit of respite. She is on a tour to see the spiritual sights, but ironically, it is here in the tiny cubicle of my dad's room that I am having the spiritual experience of my life.

I watch my 93-year-old father hover in a twilight zone between this world and the next and I wonder what holds him here. His tenacious grip on life suggests he's not yet ready to release his grasp and take that free-falling glide into the unknown. His passage will prove to be a long, slow swan's song, a kind of graceful soaring over to take a peek at the other side, with a gliding back for farewells and assurances of his love and gratitude for all he's about to leave behind. I've been soaring with him these past days, holding his hands in that mudra of connection, union and trust, as we nap and meditate, inhabiting a zone of peaceful bliss.

Yesterday we were suddenly back in the beautiful garden splendor of our South Dakota home, the paradise he created through his love affair with the earth; digging her soil, planting her seeds, bringing nature's miracles to fruition. I am five and barefooted, tan from the South Dakota summer sun. The grass is smooth and moist under my feet. I am laughing. The air is filled with colorful Midwestern birds. Dad is moving dirt in a red wheelbarrow, tanned, sweating, and clearly in bliss. The locust, elm and cottonwood trees are fully leafed out; red, pink, yellow and white roses are blooming. Everything is perfect; we are in paradise.

I meditate much of the time I'm with my dad. I ask Guan Shi Yin to help him feel peaceful and safe, so that he can find trust and a way to surrender. Old anxieties pull at his mind. When he is confused, he frets about the safety of his wallet and whether all of us here in the room have been given our own rooms "in the hotel."

I see the part of his mind that is fearful of loss, exploitation and losing control. I see the part of his mind that always took care of others and put concerns about their comfort and welfare far beyond his own. I then get to see those magical, transcendent moments when he is able to move to that space beyond the thinking mind, when he floats on the currents of peace and bliss. It is then that he is truly in harmony and balance. I long for him to be released to only those moments.

I sing the hymns and recite the prayers that I know are the mantras familiar to him from our shared spiritual lineage, hoping to help him connect with the comfort of divine energy. "Praise God from whom all blessings flow...." and "Our Father, which art in Heaven, Hallowed be Thy name, Thy kingdom come, Thy will be done, On Earth as it is in Heaven," I hold my hands in the universal mudra of prayer.

Sometimes in my meditation I see him curling up more and more until he is a tiny baby in the womb, but the womb is my central energy channel that has expanded to contain an entire world. Dad is resting comfortably in his bed, Yuan Miao's deceased Tibetan grandmother and holder of her lineage is peacefully stirring soup in a huge cauldron, singing, chanting and smiling.

Miao is a five-year-old child playing around the bedside, laughing and singing. I'm sitting in the corner in my chair feeling utter peace and tranquility, but with tears running down my face. For me there is still a strong, aching tug, deep in my being as I try to let go and let transformation from one realm to the next take place. I believe my dad and I share this sense of wanting to hold onto what we've loved, created and known so far. I'm sure it is what holds him here, even as his physical body deteriorates around him. Miao's grandmother just keeps stirring soup, smiling, and in her peaceful way indicating, "That's good. He can go, that's good. Let him rest, that's good. He will go in his own way, that's good." Such a simple, beautiful, comforting mantra, "That's good."

I love being here with "Grandma" in my meditations; the hours are timeless and beautiful. She is helping me learn another lesson in surrender and letting go.

47

Lessons in Equanimity

When my final day here in the Elizabeth Seton Residence arrives, I watch my dad lying peacefully in his bed. My prayers to Guan Yin that he might find peace, comfort, trust and the courage to surrender have been answered. His hands, which just two weeks ago were frantically twisting the bed sheets into tortured rolls, are resting calmly on the white sheets folded smoothly over the blankets. His face is serene, his mouth curves periodically to an almost-smile as he journeys on his private travels behind closed eyes. He has just finished a session of physical therapy that was excruciating to watch. He was trying with all his usual determination to follow the therapist's commands.

"Release your right hand from the top of the walker, Dr. Sattler."

Already tired from a morning's walk with me that required Herculean efforts to utilize the walker, he could not process her simple commands. I watched his fingers clutch the walker tighter in an amazingly strong grip.

"No, Dr. Sattler. Let go of the walker," the therapist repeated over and over. I could see my dad trying to follow her instructions. There was no anger, no frustration, there were just persistent, dogged, and ultimately futile attempts to comply with her requests.

After each failure, he would simply and calmly and with the greatest graciousness and equanimity say, "I'm sorry, could you repeat that?" Then he would try again. His actions spoke the mantra, "Don't stop, keep going."

As I meditate, I realize once again, he is my greatest teacher. Back home, I have been working on balancing poses in my yoga and Qigong classes. I am undeniably bad at them: I waver, I tense up, I topple, I inevitably fall over. I become embarrassed and then frustrated with myself. My lovely yoga teacher caught my attention a few weeks ago when, as we were mostly all wavering and toppling, she said, "Just observe how you respond to challenge. You are doing a challenging pose. Do you give up, get angry and frustrated, collapse in defeat? Or do you reset your course, re-center and try again, inching toward improvement?"

I have been mulling this over as I resolutely attempt to do the yoga and Qigong balancing poses. I realize I have spent the morning watching my father patiently model this lesson for me. He wavers, tenses, and topples, and then calmly re-centers, resets his course and tries again. He is the epitome of equanimity. There is no expressed frustration or anger, only unwavering persistence.

"I will try again."

He rests now from the effort, finding a perfect balance.

My father, Theodore Sattler, MD. At bottom is my niece, Meredith Walker.

48

My Teenaged Teacher

Arriving back home in California, I try again to reenter post-cancer life with my family. I now feel like the immigrant in my own life. Toby is about to enter the last semester of his senior year, having slipped through much of high school while I was commuting back and forth to Stanford, focused on chemotherapy, spiritual discovery and staying alive.

Since giving birth to him, I have been a member of the "sandwich generation." Usually that is a term used to describe those of us who have both elderly parents and young children in our care at the same time. For the past 17 years I have been squeezed between the pressures of both of their needs. I now find myself confronting a new dimension to this sandwich state. I'm now called upon to find a way to let go of both my parents and my son at the same time.

While my parents have been passing from elderly to deceased, my only child has been passing from sweet little boy who cried when I needed to leave for work, to 17 year-old, almost man, who needs for me to let him go. The process is painful for us all, like any birth or rebirth. It involves everyone releasing old forms, old identities.

For the most part, my son is ready to go. The old forms and identities shackle him, chaining him to places he's long since outgrown. Our former life and relationship are like his outgrown running shoes, pinching his toes, confining his growth until finally his feet have broken free by wearing holes all the way through at the most constraining points.

But for me, like for many moms, this passage is filled with labor pains and slow progression. I can't bear to let go of everyone at once. Even with my attempted embrace of impermanence, it seems too much to bear. My mantra is threatening to become, "I can't let go."

My son is pushing the limits like most teenagers. He wants me to fade into the background now. We have had marijuana and questionable friends and sullen, pulled-inward silences that seem to suck all the air from the room, replacing it with tension and a horrible sense of something dangerous held in, like everyone is holding his breath.

Gary and I have continually been coming across his marijuana paraphernalia. We sit up late at night discussing how to handle this. Given that Toby is a straight A student, it is difficult to make a case that it is negatively impacting school performance, but it is obvious from the array of artistic drawings of cannabis leaves decorating his walls, his growing collection of hand-blown pipes, and his secrecy that this is becoming a problem.

One day when I have had very little sleep and I am feeling particularly edgy, I come across a brand new—actually quite beautiful—hand blown glass pipe. I am waiting at the dining room table when he passes through on his way "out."

"I came across this in your room. I can only imagine you used the allowance we give you to buy it. I'm really concerned about how much of your energy is wrapped up around your relationship with pot. I'm actually now really angry about it. You'd better think long and hard"—in my anger I'm resorting to using a phrase my dad used when he was angry at my sister and me—"about going down this road and the effect it's having on your relationships with people who love you."

He looks stunned, it's obvious to him that I am barely containing a reservoir of built-up anger. "I don't think it's that big of a deal. But, OK, I'll think about it." He walks out the door. A few minutes later I see him out in the yard swinging a sledge hammer and hitting the ground over and over. He is yelling, "I'm a good person, I'm a good person," and tears are streaming down his face. Terrified that one of his upswings is going to land full on in his face, and somewhat out of control myself, I call Gary who says, "I'm in the car, I'll be right there." After some father/son car time we try to talk it through, but even though Toby and I both apologize for how we handled things, I sense a new wariness between us.

Still financially dependent on us, but apparently fed up with what he experiences as our intrusion into his private life, he decides to establish a separate base of operations and begins building a small house on the corner of our property. Fueled with a desire for independence, he gets a job at the local hardware store, studies the county building code, and even learns enough about electricity to do the wiring himself. A day comes when two friends arrive to help him move his bed and his belongings to the new location. As he heads out the door, he's looking elated and proud. He looks at me and says triumphantly, "Well, today is the day I'm moving out."

I stare at the baby pictures which seem to be everywhere in our house, trying to grasp that this baby is gone, transformed into some completely new entity. I'm still looking at pictures of my mother, trying to grasp the existential reality that she too has transformed into some energetic form I can't begin to understand. Evidence of impermanence is all around me.

I can't believe I am having so much trouble letting my son make this transition. As a therapist, I know all about separation and individuation. How many parents have I coached to let their kids go so they can one day return, transformed and ready to form a new attachment from a place of independence?

I feel like we are back in Elizabeth's Wig Salon, knowing that in a few days no matter what I do, I will be bald and vulnerable. One day soon

I will watch my son drive out the driveway on his way to college, car loaded with comforters, study lamps and skateboard. Our family will be changed forever. In the meantime, we continue to try out the new behaviors that will come with that transition.

He comes home later and later, and spends more nights away. I try to trust his ability to make good choices and resist the temptation to track his whereabouts. We are trying on wigs, playing dress up, experimenting with letting go of old identities, trying to embrace transformation and change.

I close my eyes and remember my son's chubby fingers patting my face. I remember his warm baby-body, heavy and trusting in my arms. I remember his little hand in mine as we walk from car to first day of kindergarten. I remember his face lighting up as he sees me in the crowd of mothers after school and how he runs and jumps into my arms, giving me that unrestrained, open-hearted hug of love that only a child can give his mom. I remember the cookies, the kitchen "science experiments," the feel of mud under our feet, the laughter, the wrestling and the shared wonder at our beautiful natural world, and I don't want to give any of it up. It's like losing my hair to the cancer treatment; I feel like parts of me are dropping away, a few strands at a time.

I grasp for what the cancer has taught me: my cancer dharma. Forms and incarnations have a life span. Life is movement, energy moving. If we don't let the old forms transform into other energetic states, there is no room for the new forms to arise and take their rightful place. Grasping to old forms ultimately creates disease. When movement totally ceases there is death. To transform we must surrender. The first step of surrender is to let go.

"Let go, let go, let go. That's good."

Toby, my teenage teacher.

49

Reinventing Myself

Gary looks concerned and tells me he's afraid he will not be able to pay the mortgage this month. Stunned, I realize I have no source of income. For 23 years, until the cancer diagnosis, our lifestyle was predicated on both our incomes.

An artist and a therapist, neither of us made huge amounts of money. My father and sister helped with our expenses during my cancer treatment, but Gary has single-handedly been trying to make up for my lost income ever since. For many weeks, I have been watching him come home from his full-time day job, and sit hunched in front of his computer doing free-lance work until two in the morning.

For the first time in my 58 years on the planet, I have no immediate way to come up with money. Frantic, I feel panic invading every cell. Miao often says to approach our practices with the mantra, "One hundred percent - No Doubt."

Determined to stay on my healing path, I go straight to the living room, pull out the DVD, and do all the mudras, mantras and the Yoga of Joy. As I experience my anxiety dissolving, I am grateful that such a simple mantra can remove resistance and obstacles so I am able to sit down and begin the practices when I need them. Once begun, my immediate experience of calm, clarity, balance and connection to something so much bigger than myself becomes an ongoing reason to trust the practices, "One hundred percent - No Doubt." From this calm, centered place, with my mind uncluttered by anxious thoughts, I can begin to focus on my work and money situation.

I originally envisioned six months of not working while I went through chemotherapy. That would have given me from February to the end of the summer. I then decided I wanted time to recoup my energy and get my son launched into his senior year of high school. Then there was the pressure of helping him with his college applications and financial aid forms.

A part of me began to realize I was stalling. I really did not want to return to my old way of holding a space for people in pain. I had come to realize that the way, as a deeply empathetic person, I previously absorbed their pain may have felt relieving to them, but it had the potential to be damaging to me. Having spent the past year intricately repairing my body, my energy, my psyche, my very soul, and still feeling so fragile, I was afraid to expose myself to toxic environments of any kind. Literally buying more time, I cashed in one of my few retirement investments, saying I needed to wait to resume work until after the holidays.

On New Years Day, I had a major meltdown, shedding many tears and grieving that I would have to send myself back into the environment that I now believed contributed to my illness. Gary agreed to use his bonus (which had been intended to go into our son's college fund) to usher us through January to February.

So here we are, almost exactly one year from when I stood in the post office with my "leave of absence" letters in hand. Now, instead of giddy and elated, I feel frantic, teary and overwhelmed. How could I possibly have arrived at a place where I feel so lost, confused and yes, stymied at figuring out my direction in life? I have two master's degrees, two professional licenses and I am on Craigslist looking for jobs. I need to generate money, but I need a break from the intense responsibility of the helping profession jobs I've always had. I don't know how to reassemble my life.

I know my old way of working hard and trying to control outcome worked to a point, but then it had some pretty high costs. The end result was exhaustion and probably a compromised immune system. But I haven't been able to design a new way of working. I am trying to trust, to stay on a new path and to have courage. In fact, I feel terrified and I am beginning to doubt the entire path. "One hundred percent - No Doubt" is giving way to, "I can't do it!" I find myself trying to make peace with going back to working as a psychotherapist exactly the way I did it before, which seems so familiar and rational.

For the past month I have gotten nowhere trying to find a job teaching in Kaiser Hospital's Health Education Department, the local junior college, or even hospice. So, that's how, out of desperation, I am now looking on Craigslist, amusing myself with possibilities like Welfare Fraud Investigator, Sign Spinner, Part time Driver Assistant for Live Snake Program, Skunk and Rat Abatement, and Clean, Legit Tattoo Artist. I find I can make $50.00 for a half-hour match in a "friendly, tasteful women's wrestling video." (I swear I have not made this up.)

Transformation calls on me to move beyond my old identity, my old familiar ways of being in the world, but I am a novice here. Trying to grasp the concepts that Yuan Miao has thrown out to me, I remember courage, trust, faith, surrender, but how do I use them to redesign a life? I am Gretel in the child's story, *Hansel and Gretel,* desperately trying to leave a trail of bread crumbs to follow back to my old life as I travel deeper and deeper into an unknown forest.

50

The Qigong Master

Discovering that I need some anchor in my life, I cling to Miao's practices. "It's the main course, it's not dessert," she has stressed again and again. Deciding to begin my day with the main course even now that chemotherapy is over (although I am actually feeling I should be spending every second finding a job), I reestablish my daily ritual of sitting on the golden brown carpet of our living room in front of my laptop that is glowing with Miao's DVD. I decide to adopt the Nike mantra of "Just Do It," even though I know they're trying to sell me shoes.

Faithfully twining my fingers into mudras, I chant the mantras, and visualize colors to positively affect eleven different conditions of body, mind or spirit such as blood pressure, cardiovascular health, mood, or nerve health. I then practice the entire Yoga of Joy and sit for at least 20 minutes of meditation before setting out on my daily activity.

Glowing with openly flowing energy, I am definitely "in the vibration." However, I still do not have gainful employment. I am feeling steadily richer in spirit as I become steadily poorer financially. "Trust," I hear Miao intoning. "Trust and courage. Surrender." It is hard to trust; I still am not even sure what I am trusting. I am afraid this new way of being is going to get me into serious trouble.

Miao is gone traveling and teaching during much of this time, and I begin to study with a Qigong master I've met who is also from China. Qigong is a 5,000-year-old healing art which activates life energy (*Qi*) for self-healing and the healing of others. I volunteer to sell the master's products at one of his workshops in exchange for the enrollment fee, and aglow with expanded energy and light, I am suddenly the world's greatest salesperson. Everyone seems to want to purchase a CD or a DVD. I am not even surprised when I receive a call from him the next day asking if I would like to work for him. This is a first experience of how "living in the vibration" will change my life.

Agreeing to do the marketing and promotion for the first-ever large event he wants to do in Berkeley, I begin the first job I have ever had for which I essentially have no formal training or experience. I have never taken a marketing or business class in my life. Living in the world of energy cultivation, my Qigong teacher has recognized my expanded energy field and hired me based on my essential inner nature, my blue pearl, my *mani*. There would be no way to describe this part of myself on a resumé, but here is validation from the external world that it is real and visible to at least one person trained to see it.

But transformation can be a slow process. A month later, I am chewing my finger nails as I try to write a press release that captures the essence of my Qigong teacher, while I fume about the delay in a return call from the head of the Transpersonal Psychology Department of my alma mater, whom I hope to convince to host a free, evening pre-workshop event. My table is littered with wadded-up sheets from a yellow legal pad, screaming the phone numbers, email addresses and workshop assignments for an army of volunteers I am trying to recruit, train and organize. What has happened to all the golden light?

Without even realizing it, I have gone back to my old habits: my nose is set to the grindstone; I am obsessing, worrying, overdoing, and creating stress for myself and for everyone around me. "I'm afraid," is a constant refrain. In psychological terms, I have again found a way to bind my energy to anxiety and worry, a very old pattern. With workaholism in full throttle, my ego is fully engaged: I am determined to control a successful outcome for this event.

51

'Don't Stop—
Keep Going'

Every other week I drive the old red Taurus through masses of BMWs, Mercedes and Lexuses belonging to the successful, golden people of Marin County commuting home from work. Crossing the parking lot of the Mill Valley Community Center, my step is slower, energy dimmer: Miao has been away for several months and a dwindling number of us "Pearls" are trying to carry on in her absence.

Tonight five of us sit on what I suddenly notice are actually very hard metal folding chairs. It is difficult to carry on without her and to figure out how to be self-reliant. How do we stay confidently on the path without being supported by the physical presence of our teacher? Trying to recreate the feel of her presence, someone has put her "Love" CD in a boom box and we meditate while listening to her mantric singing. Surfacing from meditation, I realize I am afraid the group is going to eventually disappear.

Driving home, encapsulated in my little red Midwestern car, my brain activated by the strobe-light effect of oncoming traffic, I suddenly hear Miao saying clearly, "Spiritual practice should not only be a personal refuge, but a service to others." Arriving home, in a pivotal moment of my spiritual journey, I send the following email to the main organizer of our group:

> **From:** Susan Sattler
> **Date:** March 17, 2008, 7:26 PM
> **Subject:** Loving Tara
>
> ---
>
> I've been thinking a lot about the Blue Pearl Group since last meeting and about how I can take some responsibility for helping us make the transformation to the next form.
>
> Focusing on what I have learned from Miao that has been instrumental in my healing, I see that there are specific practices and then general ways of orienting myself to life. Two of the practices that I think are bottom-line essential are the mudras and the mantras.
>
> I believe that a big part of what healed me was staying in that optimal vibration that Miao talks about. Actually DOING the mudras on her DVD and CHANTING the mantras with her were key. I would be willing to try to teach/lead us in doing those specific mudras and chanting the mantras, but I don't know how Miao feels about someone else leading the mantras. I am sure much of the healing is about chanting the mantras with her - matching our voice to her vibration.
>
> However, I think that it is time for me to step forward out of the "student only wanting to receive" role, and into more of a "teacher, willing to share what I've learned" role.

With this email I slip out of another skin and slither over a threshold into a new realm.

The following night I have a dream in which I see Miao and she is pregnant. I am thinking, "Isn't she a little old to be pregnant?" But she is beautiful.

A couple of weeks later, standing at the front of the Blue Pearl room, I am sweating into the only Chinese-like article of clothing I possess: a blue silk jacket I have selected for this first night of teaching mudras and mantras. Having been assured that since my heart is in the right place it is fine to teach these practices, I now stand before six people whom I know are longing for Miao. Demonstrating the mudra and instructing which colors to visualize are easy: chanting the mantra is frankly terrifying.

My monkey mind and ego are having a heyday: "These people don't want to hear you do the mantras, they want Miao. You were never a great singer anyway. You shouldn't be chanting mantras, you are not the recipient of this lineage."

Trying to focus on the syllables and tones, I sweat my way through the experience, remembering a horrible event years ago when my father invited me to give a talk on eating disorders to a group of doctors at his medical clinic. Only an intern at the time, but not wanting to disappoint him, I agreed and sweated my way through that experience with debilitating cottonmouth making it all but impossible for me to speak.

But the Pearls have learned their lessons well: they are loving, kind and compassionate, encouraging me to continue.

For the next class, I bring a long, rectangular piece of light blue cardboard on which I have printed *Namo Nan Gala Om Ah Hum* in black magic marker. From Miao's DVD I have learned that this is the mantra that is used to regulate blood pressure. Wanting to help everyone understand how this mantra could be helpful on a daily basis I remind them, "We all know that when we are stressed or angry our blood pressure tends to go up. This is a practice you can use to regulate that. Sometimes if I am stuck in traffic I'll just sit in my car and chant the mantra. But here, let me show you the mudra that goes with it—you can do that if you are stuck in traffic too."

I'm feeling more comfortable and confident as I utilize my training as a teacher. It's fun to use all the senses and to provide opportunities for people who learn in various ways, auditorily, visually, and kinaesthetically. I move around the room, helping each person entwine their fingers. I have chosen this as our first mudra because it is practical and a relatively simple one to do. I then hold up three pieces of satin fabric, purple, sepia and light yellow: the colors we need to visualize. Doing the mudra, mantra and color visualization all at the same time, we practice lowering our blood pressure.

When the night of Miao's return finally arrives, I have been teaching mudras and mantras for two months. I enter the Blue Pearl room and see her dressed in beautiful red silk, playing her Chinese harp. Electric with her energy, the room seems to shimmer and to be filled with light. My mind is empty as I drift on the currents of her voice and mantric singing.

Somewhere very far away I hear her saying, "Loving Tara (the name she has chosen to call me) will teach you a mudra and mantra now."

I am a witness, seeing myself from some distant vantage point, helping everyone twine their fingers into the heart-function-supporting mudra. "*Namo Zhun Ti So Ha*," we chant strongly. There is no sweat, no cottonmouth, no wavering tone, no monkey mind terrorizing me; I know that somehow Miao is lending us her connection to an elevated state of consciousness.

The group is ending and in altered states we mill about, socializing. Miao comes up to me, locks me in her expanded-consciousness stare and says, "You have touched my heart. You are Grandma's granddaughter too. I will teach you the lineage. We will teach together one day, but not now because you have a family to take care of. I saw you offering healing energy when you were teaching the mudra. You are different now as Loving Tara than you were as Susan, and you will be different again as a bodhisattva. Don't stop. Keep going."

"Don't stop. Keep going." The same words spoken by the Lakota Sioux medicine man, swirling around my head and echoing beyond the sweat lodge out across the South Dakota prairie that mystical night so many years ago.

The next night I have a vivid dream. Miao and I are with a pregnant woman. The woman is unconscious, but Miao and I have to deliver the baby. Miao says to just follow her. She does some mudras over the woman that I follow as well as I can, and then she says, "It's time," and she reaches into the woman and pulls out a baby and hands it to me. I am wiping mucous out of its mouth and notice she has reached in again and has pulled out a second baby that she is now tending to. We are both preoccupied with new-born babies when I wake up.

52

Surrender

Throughout this time I have been continuing to organize the Berkeley Qigong event. On a chilly Bay Area June day, Gary and I fill our aging Toyota van with flowers, flyers, table cloths and Qigong products and set out across the Richmond Bridge to Berkeley. Standing at the entrance to the International House, which has hosted multi-cultural events since the 1930s, I greet men and women of all ages who are hoping for the healing which my Qigong master has defined as positive change. Our goal was to have 150 participants. 160 now sit eagerly anticipating the master's appearance on stage.

By the end of the weekend everyone is glowing with enhanced energy, attacking the product tables like locusts, and signing up for future retreats, classes and workshops. By most standards, the event is a great success. Only I know in my heart that I have accomplished my part in this production in the old way, the busy way, the "heart death" way, the cancer way. I have not yet fully integrated the courage, trust, surrender and faith necessary to work and live in a new way; I am still learning how to do that. I know that I am at a choice-point.

Two weeks after the workshop, I meet with my Qigong teacher and resign from my "marketing career." It is an ultimate act of surrender: an attempt to drive a stake into the heart of my old way of working hard to control outcome. I'm hoping this will be the last time I work in this way. Theoretically, I could do this job, any job really, in a new way with more trust, less control, but I know I won't, because my old habits are still so entrenched and still so able to assure my ego it will get what it wants. I have to surrender because I haven't yet fully let go of control, and integrated trust into my life.

I am still grappling with the question of what does one trust when letting go of fear. Since I can't control how this transformation unfolds, I have to trust some wisdom beyond my conscious cognitive understanding to guide me, and that apparently requires me to stay in an unformed state, without a job, a bit longer.

And yes, not knowing where my next income may come from, I am still terrified about money. "Trust. Courage. Faith. Surrender." Paging through my journal for inspiration, I find this quote from Miao. "When we are focused on fears about our survival, we lose our power. Service. Commit your life to service; have passion about that. Have courage! When you are on fire, your passion will burn obstacles. When we focus on that energy, survival will take care of itself."

I am trying to make my peace with not worrying about survival. After all, I am supposed to be keeping my nose to the grindstone. I want to believe that if I surrender my desire to control outcome and follow my passionate energy, survival will take care of itself. But do I really believe it? What if I follow this teaching and end up a bag lady under the bridge?

And then, clear as day, I hear a voice in my mind saying, "Remember the bank night raffle." I sit up suddenly. This is a family story about my father that perfectly illustrates Miao's teaching.

I think my dad knew he wanted to become a doctor from the time his father collapsed and died of that fatal heart attack, but circumstances were stacked against him. The youngest of six kids, he was left to grow up in a family with essentially no money. He was 15 years old in 1929 when drought swept across the Midwest, eventually creating the Dust Bowl. Crops failed, the stock market crashed, and banks closed. By the time he was 18 and graduating from high school, there were bread lines, soup kitchens and despair across much of the country.

But my dad was smart, hardworking and passionate. He wanted a life of service: he wanted to be a doctor. Having landed a job at the local drugstore, he had the courage to apply to the fine old liberal arts college in town, and commit to working 60 hours a week as a soda jerk, hoping to eventually be given more responsibilities in the pharmacy. Taking all the science and math the college could offer, he trusted that somehow he would go to medical school.

From a survival-fear perspective, he had no right to think that could happen. He was barely able to meet his undergraduate tuition and operating expenses by continuing to live at home with his mother. Medical school tuition was much more expensive; he would have to live away from home, and he knew the demands of the curriculum would not allow him to work nearly as many hours even if he could find a job. There were no student loans in those days.

With his passion burning away obstacles, he applied to medical school, was admitted, and he accepted, without any idea of how he would solve the myriad problems on the practical plane: primarily the need for money.

And then, the one movie theater in town, the Dakota Theater, instituted something called "Bank Night." People would buy raffle tickets, something like today's lottery tickets, and periodically there would be a drawing with the winner taking home all the cash. My dad never had any available cash, so he had never purchased a ticket.

Late one night as they were washing up the counters of the soda bar, the old druggist started in, "Come on, Ted, what do we have to lose? I'll make you a deal. We each buy one ticket. If you win, give me 50 dollars.

If I win, I'll give you 50 dollars."

"Sorry, Mr. Wallbaum, I can't do that. I'm not making my tuition payments as it is. The college had to let me defer payment again this semester."

"Come on, the tickets barely cost anything, Ted. Everyone's doing it. You might even win."

With a sigh, my dad gave the old druggist a wry smile and reached for his wallet, knowing all too well his boss's persistence would eventually prevail.

Weeks later, having forgotten all about it since he was always working on Friday nights and couldn't attend the drawings at the theater, my dad was startled by the sound of his best friend Joe pounding on the window of the drugstore to be let in. Friends were streaming across the street behind him. Agitated and breathless, Joe was gesticulating wildly, "You won, Ted, you won! They drew your name right out of the raffle cage. You have to be there in person to claim it. You only have ten minutes to get there."

In shock, my dad said, "There's a half hour left 'til closing. I can't leave."

Swarms of people surrounded him, lifted him up and were beginning to carry my protesting dad out of the drugstore. "Don't worry," called Joe, "I'm great at wiping down counters." It could have been a scene right out of *It's a Wonderful Life,* with Jimmy Stewart supported by the whole town.

We'll never know if pure, simple good fortune shone on my dad that night, or if the town fathers intervened through some community sleight of hand. But either way, just like Miao promises, a piece of survival took care of itself. "One hundred percent - No Doubt!" A passionate young man, committed to service, found that the Bank Night winnings were just enough to cover his first year's expenses for medical school.

53

Discovering the Secret

Strangely, although I have not done any outreach to resurrect my former psychotherapy practice, I begin to receive a few calls for appointments—not from my most recent clients, but from people who have been referred to me by colleagues, people who were clients long ago, and people who know me in other ways.

Sitting back in my tan leather therapist's chair, occasionally glancing out the second story bay window that gives me a view of the treetops, I listen to Mary describe her rage upon discovering her husband has been having an affair. Financially dependent on him and the mother of two small children, she is afraid and confused. My mind is not racing ahead, searching for the perfect understanding of her family of origin or the perfect therapeutic intervention. My mind is quiet and still, spacious and open. I realize I am holding a state of consciousness within which my client can explore what is going on with her, experience my compassion and lack of judgment, and maybe even find her own way to trust, faith, courage and surrender. In this oceanic state, I find helpful therapeutic insights and understandings about where she may be stuck floating into my awareness, but it is all effortless, like swimming in a peaceful ocean and watching insight float by. I can reach out and catch what is useful if I want; I can also choose to let it float on by.

My Qigong teacher has taught me that there are two levels of energy: the universal *qi* field and the informational level of energy. "We need to be clear about our *purpose*," he has stressed. "Our purpose will guide us to the informational level of energy." Floating in my second-story office, my blue carpet the ocean beneath my client and me, I realize I know what he means. Having surrendered my old way of working hard as the therapist, I know how to stay in the universal energy field and I am beginning to trust that what I need on the informational level of energy will come to me if I wait, if I have trust, courage and faith.

I am seeing very few clients, but I am doing it in a new way. I have the startling revelation that when I am in this clear, focused, vast consciousness—free of mental chatter and limiting concepts—everything I need to make choices and achieve my purpose will be available to me. This is what I can trust and within which I understand why Miao's practices need to be the main course, not dessert: they train my mind to hold this state of consciousness and awareness. Feeling giddy, I realize I have just begun to understand a secret.

54

Teaching the Lineage

In the meantime, my son has graduated from high school, my father is slipping further into states of confusion as he straddles the line between this realm and whatever comes next, and summer is racing by. I awake from another vivid dream. I am with Miao, and Gary is there too. We walk out to a very busy street and are talking. A car zooms past very fast, almost hitting her. I guide her with my arms to the side of the road. I am shielding her from the cars, encircling her with my arms the way a mother would a small child.

In my dream, she says, "This is a horrible country."

I say, "I know, let's go to yours."

She says, "If I asked you to come, would you come?"

I hesitate for a moment and say, "Yes, I would come."

She says, "We can go for my birthday."

* * *

In September, just before the Second Annual World Music Celebration of Universal Healing, Miao reveals precipitously that after the concert the Mill Valley Blue Pearl Group will no longer be meeting.

Just like that, the old form dissolves. Impermanence. Courage, trust, faith, surrender. I want to be strong, embracing even this change with an attitude of "That's good," but I am totally thrown off by this news. Miao has been my rock, my anchor. The Blue Pearl Group meetings have been a primary organizing factor in my life. The first thing on my priority list has been the group, and any opportunity to be with Miao. Even as I had been listening to her teachings on impermanence, marveling at what an indisputable reality this is, I was securely tucking this Wednesday night Blue Pearl Group into my schedule book, certain it had become a permanent part of my life.

After the concert, struggling with my fear that I will never see her again, I decide that my best chance to stay connected in some way is to continue the practices she has taught us, which have been a reliable touchstone in my life now for several years. Practicing faithfully every day, trying to stay in that boundless, expanded consciousness, I am sometimes reduced to tears, and sometimes imbued with a sense of infinite love.

Later in September, I have my one-year-out CT scan and am told I am still in complete remission, my son leaves home for college, and the Blue Pearl Group has its final meeting. Another big tilt of the pinball machine: game over, whatever comes next will be a brand new game.

Two months later I receive a phone call inviting me to a teaching, hike and dinner with Miao. The next day, as if in a dream, four of us "Pearls" are walking with Miao through the December mist on a bay tree-lined trail on Mount Tamalpais, a 2,500-foot mountain in Marin County that is an outdoor haven for urban San Franciscans. Slipping over the rain slicked rocks and muddy trail, I try to keep pace with Miao as she seems to fly down the trail with her usual fearless abandon.

"How is your father?" she throws over her shoulder.

Surprised that she is asking a question about what could be considered the mundane, practical plane, I find myself telling her things we've never discussed before. "My father spent his life caring for others," I pant. "He is a doctor, but he is more than that: he is a healer. There are many people who not only admire, but love him. It is so difficult to accept and understand that he should have to spend his final years adjusting to blindness. He has beautiful, sensitive hands. I know that they somehow help him heal people."

Images of the preacher at the revival meeting my grandfather attended on the South Dakota prairie float through my mind. I am remembering the testimonials of miraculous healings when he "laid on hands" that day. My father had an excellent Western medical education at Northwestern University Medical School, and I know the knowledge he received there was critical to his success as a physician; but there was also his deep compassion and those beautiful, sensitive fingers, sensing things beyond words or cognitive understanding.

"I am just realizing that my healing lineage comes through my father."

"That is why you like to use your hands and to practice the mudras. It is in your DNA."

We have arrived at a grassy knoll with a spacious view; San Francisco Bay stretches across the horizon. The Bay Bridge is draped between San Francisco and Oakland, a delicate fringe adorning a rippling light blue expanse of silk, covered with tiny triangles of pure white sails.

"*Om Mani Padme Hum.*" We are twirling, lifting arms to the sky, bending and swaying like the trees all around us. We are laughing, bumping into one another, joyous children rolling down the hill. Exhausted and breathless we collect ourselves, find a cross legged position and begin to quiet our minds.

Eventually I find my way back up the hill to a small bench overlooking the view. The others are still below me, absorbed in their meditation. Appearing next to me, Miao turns and says, "I want you to begin to teach a class of your own. I've asked you this before. You can do the mudras and mantras. It is important to spread the lineage. It does not matter if you only have one student; if one benefits from your teaching, that is good."

Later when I tell Gary about this exchange, he says, "I will come to your class. I will be your one student, even if no one else shows up."

I'm remembering another thing the Lakota medicine man told me all those years ago as we sat on his steps and looked out across the South Dakota prairie. "If a medicine man helps you, you have a responsibility to the spirits which you must fulfill within a year's time. You can do that by doing something for the people, to help the people. We have the "giveaway." I know a family whose son was dying and he was helped to heal by the Great Spirit and his family happily gave away all they had to help the people. Value is in the family and love, not in the material world."

On the first Tuesday in January, determined to fulfill Miao's request and my responsibility to the spirits, I walk across the cork floor of the yoga studio I have rented for the evening, surrounded by photographs of Buddhas, lotus flowers and bamboo. Gary is sitting in the center of a small semi-circle of folding chairs. He is flanked by one member of the Blue Pearl Group, one of my closest girlfriends, my stepdaughter and her husband, and two women new to my life who have signed up for the class.

It is my debut teaching the lineage passed down to me from Miao. Teaching this class, I move well beyond the short mudra/mantra lessons I was giving as part of the Blue Pearl Groups. This is an hour and a half class and I am the teacher. I lead a guided visualization which takes us into meditation. As we exit the meditation I hand out paper and crayons that are the colors we will visualize as we do the endocrine balancing mudra and mantra. "Just enjoy coloring. There are no rules, you do not have to do anything realistic unless you want to." I show them the mudra, we chant the mantra: *Damo Da Hum Hum*. We do a Sword of Wisdom exercise from Miao's Yoga of Joy designed to improve balance and to help us practice focusing even in the midst of distractions, supporting us to move through obstacles and illusions. At the end we are dancing around the room, smiling and honoring Miao's example of staying connected to joy.

As I teach, she is traveling and teaching internationally. Smiling, I remember the dream of Miao and me, delivering, and then holding, two newborn babies. I hear Lakota drumbeats far, far away.

Teaching the lineage.

55

The Invitation

Three weeks later something miraculous happens. I am out on our deck watering potted pansies and marigolds, thinking about the open invitation to visit our home that I extended to Miao before she left on her travels. I'm wondering if she would ever consider visiting us. In the background of my thoughts, I hear the phone ringing.

"Hello?"

"Loving Tara, this is Fay. We are back from traveling and Miao would like to come visit your loving home for a few days. There will be four of us: Miao, me, Saturn, and our friend Angela. Is that too many?"

"Of course not. You are all welcome in our home. This is a wonderful surprise."

I know there is no way to express how blessed and honored I feel that such holy, evolved beings will be with us in our home.

A few days later, I watch from my front step as they tumble out of their white mini-van like schoolchildren, quickly inspect their surroundings, and make a bee-line for the old, rickety trampoline left over from my son's childhood days. Moments later Miao is flying eight feet above the trampoline, as she jumps harder, trying for a "better ride." Running toward the trampoline, I have a moment of feeling just like I did when my son and his friends were little: what fun it looks like they are having, and oh, my god, they're going to fly off and kill themselves. But I see the look of pure joy and fearlessness on Miao's face, and I find myself joining them on the trampoline. We are all like popcorn bouncing around, laughing, jumping, falling, rolling. I am eight years old again. I have to shake my head and pinch myself to believe that I am jumping on our trampoline with my enlightened Chinese/Tibetan teacher.

The visit unfolds with dreamlike energy. Flowing from one activity to the next, we follow no preset schedule. I'm reminded of the long, lazy summer days of my childhood when my sister and I and our friend from down the road would entertain ourselves all day. We would follow one activity until we were bored, and then someone would have a new idea. We would ride our horses awhile, play bakery with mud pies, put on our swimsuits and jump in the sprinklers, even read in the shade of a big elm tree.

Now the time with Miao has that same free-flowing feeling. This is the gift of letting go of Busy. We go for a walk down our country road. Upon our return, Fay discovers the musical instruments in our living room. Suddenly she is playing a wooden flute, Miao is playing the piano, Angela and I are shaking maracas and we are all dancing around the room singing *Om Mani Padme Hum*. Plopping down on the floor, we do some spontaneous moves from the Yoga of Joy. It feels like the old days, before computers and video games and structured camps to keep kids busy while both parents work. I'm loving playing with my friends.

"The tradition of Vajrayana Buddhism in Tibet is a joyous practice," Miao says. "Of course, there is serious devotional practice, but when families gather there is singing, dancing, laughter and they're often playing bells, flutes and drums."

I'm lying on the floor, face down. Fay is massaging my back. "When I was in college, kids my age were longing for this," I remark. "Lots of us learned to play guitars and we would sit around in living rooms or barns and play and sing. We would dance too, and cook and laugh. It seems like we don't do that so much anymore." (I'm thinking, "Yes, because we're all now too busy!") "Now when we do get together, people are more likely to talk in small groups. It's not as much fun."

By the morning of the third day, I no longer think about time or what we are going to do next. I'm completely in the present moment, ready for anything. I luxuriate in the poses and meditations as Fay leads us through a practice of the Yoga of Joy. And then reality takes an even greater tilt when Miao turns to me and says, "On my next trip to China, you will come with me. You can help many people."

Just like in my dream, all I can say is, "Yes, I will come."

Miao's visits were always accompanied by playful activity.

Yuan Miao hangs Tibetan prayer flags on our property.

56

Outwitting Death

A month later I am pulling my red scarf tight around my neck and dodging speeding cars as I try to cross a street outside the Boston hotel where I am attending a writer's conference. I feel instinctively that it was a good decision to come to this particular conference. It will allow me to spend a night in my 25-year-old niece's hip apartment in Boston's South End, and then in a couple of days tag on a visit to my father who is still at my sister's home in a Boston suburb. She is away at a conference in Los Angeles, so I will keep him company.

My niece and I are laughing as we walk up the steep wooden stairs to her apartment, because I am trying to extract my ringing cell phone from my bag while preventing all my other bags from tumbling down the stairs. "Susan, this is Teresa, your father's caregiver. Your daddy, he is not responsive, I think you need to come here."

A half hour later, standing by the home hospital bed in Ann's house, I see what Teresa means by non-responsive. Eyes open, staring straight ahead, my father is obviously conscious, but not responsive in any way—so strange for a man who spent his life in motion. He does not blink, move or speak.

"Hi, Dad, it's Susan, how are you doing?"

His only granddaughter, Meredith, holds a special place in his heart. She adds her greeting that normally causes a huge smile to spread across his face, "Hi, Grandpa, it's Meredith." No response. Checking his pulse, I find it is steady and regular and he is breathing normally. I can only imagine that he has had a debilitating stroke. Minutes later, I am once again following an ambulance to the emergency room, just as I did with my mother four-and-a-half years ago. I am clinging to the mantra, "No Fear. That's good."

The emergency room doctor is quizzing us about the timing of this event when my dad suddenly says quite clearly, "Yes, that would be very nice," apparently responding to Meredith's boyfriend who has just whispered in his ear, "When you get out of here, Dr. Sattler, we'll have to have a chocolate milkshake." Explaining that a clot or "sludge" must have just passed on through a vessel, clearing the blockage, the emergency room doc admits my dad for observation overnight.

Hunched over in a recliner, huddled under a white hospital blanket a nurse has kindly given me, I spend the night watching over my beautiful father, marveling that this event has occurred when I am actually here on the East Coast, able to get to him in a quick half-hour. Another "coincidence." Remembering my last vigil with him more than a year ago at the Sister's of Charity Residence Home, I wonder if this time we will visit the edge again where one leaps off from this world into the unknown. A part of me hopes that if it comes to that, this time he will be able to surrender and take that leap, but I know his mantra has been, "I don't want to go." By morning he seems to be doing so well that I return to Boston for the final day of my workshop, and later go to my sister's home to get a full night's rest in a real bed.

Having returned on a red eye flight from Los Angeles, Ann is gently shaking me awake. "We just got a call from the hospital. Dad has taken a turn for the worse."

Entering the tiny hospital room where I had watched him rest so peacefully just the night before, we see a swarm of medical personnel gathered around his bed.

"Your dad has developed a serious pneumonia, would you like us to call a chaplain for you?"

Stunned, my sister and I are temporarily speechless. What could have happened?

"The stroke apparently damaged his swallowing ability and we think he is aspirating food and drink. This is probably an aspiration pneumonia, but now he is gravely ill. Given his age and likelihood of further strokes we assume you would not want to intervene."

Not want to intervene? My mind is racing. I look to my doctor sister and can see her medical mind is working, doing her own assessment, considering options. Bottom line is, what would my father want? We are his medical proxies. I never before fully appreciated the magnitude of that responsibility.

Huddled in the hallway under the glare of artificial lights, watching blue scrubs-clad nurses pushing carts of medical supplies, Ann and I try to make our best decision. Is it our job to help him let go or help him hang on? He has been happy living with my sister, seeing his grandchildren and having regular visits from me. He has consistently demonstrated a desire to live. We decide that at this point he would still want us to intervene if no Herculean interventions had to be made.

"We want you to try antibiotics: give them through an IV if you have to."

The doctors are clearly displeased, thinking this is *our* inability to let go of him. They obviously think we may be taking away this opportunity for him to make a final exit before some possibly not fatal, but still catastrophic event occurs. Moving my dad into a private room, which is what they do when someone is about to die, they demonstrate that they think it is unlikely he will survive. But they miscalculate what Ann and I know all too well about my father: he has a strong will to live and he is used to using his will to accomplish what he wants. "I can do it."

Three days later I am in the back of an ambulance, holding his hand and trying to reassure him as he is transported to an acute care skilled-nursing facility. He has responded well to the antibiotics, and his doctors hope he will improve enough with this level of care to recover his previous level of function. In his new room, my sister and I, my niece and my nephew are giving high fives. It seems that his Midwestern "work hard and you will prevail" ethic has worked again, seeming to fly in the face of, "You can't control everything that happens:" the old family belief system making a last stand against a new reality.

Having decided it is safe to go back to Ann's house and spend a night in a real bed again, I climb the back staircase from her spacious family room to the little attic room which was always the place where my mom and dad stayed when they visited her. My parents' energy is all around me.

I sink down on the bed thinking how strange it will be when they are both gone. Along with my sister, they are the two people in the world who have been a constant part of my entire life. Impermanence. Even after all these years under Miao's guidance, I am not sure I am ready for this. I know that when the old form dissolves a new one will arise to take its place, but right now I can't imagine even a hint of what life without them might be like.

Hoping to distract myself from this line of thought, I open my computer to check my messages. An email from Fay leaps out at me. There is a one line message:

"Miao has picked the date for the trip to China. Miao and I have booked our tickets already. This is for your reference. XOXOXO"

Attached is an itinerary for a United Airlines flight from San Francisco International Airport leaving at 11:13 a.m.. on Sunday, June 14 and arriving at Peking International Airport in Beijing on Monday, June 15 at 2:40 p.m. I don't even hesitate. I enter United's website and book my ticket: this is definitely the main course; it's not dessert.

57

What Are the Steps?

We spend the next four days spooning thickened apple juice, thickened orange juice, even thickened ice cream into my father's mouth, desperately trying to outsmart his damaged swallowing muscles. Losing weight and becoming more and more frail from inactivity, he props himself up in the hospital bed, willingly letting the physical therapist lift his emaciated leg, bend his knee and straighten the leg, the last gasp of a body that spent a lifetime doing physical work in his garden paradise: planting trees, raking leaves, weeding a large vegetable garden, and even hoisting a fifty foot chain over a branch to make a tire swing for his children and grandchildren.

"Just one more bend of the knee, Dr. Sattler," the physical therapist is saying.

Never complaining, his response is always, "Thank you so much, you're very kind." I realize this is one of my dad's primary mantras, "You're very kind." That vibration shaped his worldview. Confirming the Lakota belief that everything is circular, it is, of course, my dad who has always been very kind.

But his doctor is clearly concerned, "Your father is not able to get enough food and hydration without aspirating."

On the fourth day, she stops me in the hallway. "Your father has developed another pneumonia. His body is not fully recovered from the last bout. He is not safe to eat. This will keep happening because he is aspirating his food."

Rapidly, my father's lungs are filling up with mucous, creating an awful rasping sound when he breathes. Much of the time he is confused and agitated, asking about his long-ago deceased brothers and sisters, but in his lucid moments he demands, "What are the steps? Tell me the steps I need to take."

I know what he means: "Tell me what I have to do to control what is happening and I will gamely do it." I am reduced to weeping outside his room, realizing that he is at the end of the usefulness of the steps he has known and counted on all his physical life. He is at the end of that physical life; game over. Whatever comes next will be a new game.

In a moment of clarity I realize that I know the steps he needs now; Miao has been teaching them to me for more than five years: courage, trust, faith, surrender. I know these are not the steps my father is talking about; he is expecting the steps that will outwit death. Gently taking his hand, I shed another skin and slither into the role of guide to my father as he peers once more over the edge into the unknown.

It's time to surrender. We can't control everything that happens, certainly not at the end of life.

"You can let go, dad. You can trust. Look for the light. Have faith in all of the love. It's alright, you can let go. You can do this, just like you did all the many other adventures in your life. You can let go."

My sister, my nephew, my niece and I are sitting in rumpled clothes around my father's bed, having kept vigil for the past twenty-four hours. It is April 11th in Boston. Although the two previous weeks have sported glorious spring weather, as I look out my father's window I see that it is snowing; beautiful soft white flakes, floating in an effortless dance and covering the world with white. I have a deep sense that my father's spirit is passing; he has surrendered. That night, at one hour past midnight on Easter Sunday, he completely lets go.

End. End of life. Once again my father is my greatest teacher, finding the courage, faith and trust to surrender to the unknown. In this generation a father and his two daughters slither out of their skins together. There is no tragedy calling on the next generation to transform. Transformation happens smoothly as, recognizing that we can't always control what happens, we hold hands in one last mudra, and fly.

58

But Will We Be Poor?

I am concentrating on not losing my footing and keeping my eye on Miao's yellow jacket and her long dark braid swaying behind her as we scramble over loose rock toward a small, ragged cave opening in Wu Tai Mountain, one of the four sacred Buddhist mountains in China, about a seven-hour bus ride from Beijing. Holy people, sages and mystics have meditated in these caves for thousands of years. Wu Tai Mountain is particularly sacred because Manjusri, the bodhisattva of wisdom and pure awareness (often represented carrying a sword which cuts through illusion), is said to have meditated and taught here.

Reaching the cave entrance, I have a sudden flash of that long-ago night with the Sioux medicine man and the sweat lodge on my native South Dakota prairie. Once again, we have formed a line to enter sacred space: 18 beautiful Asian beings with straight dark hair, one western man with curly, dark brown hair, and one grown woman with hair no longer blonde, but now pure silvery white.

Entering the small rocky opening, we progress through a rough tunnel, and arrive in a large cavern, easily forty feet tall, with grey natural stone floor and walls. In the dim light I am surprised to see an altar, at least twelve feet long, on which sits a two-foot-tall marble Buddha draped in red and gold silk and flanked by tiny vases with full bouquets of flowers. Before him are candles and several smaller statues of Buddhas and bodhisattvas, including one of Guan Yin. A long hanging of slightly shiny clay-colored cloth drapes from the roof of the cave, forms a cover for the altar, and continues to the floor. Three large panels with earth-tone paintings of holy beings adorn the drape.

I am mesmerized by a red silk cloth, hanging from the ceiling, which is cut into intricate flowing designs with lotus flowers made of pink and green satin. Another red silk banner with Chinese characters and a pink lotus flows down the center of the altar. Every cell in my body is vibrating with the energy of the cave.

As I settle in to a cross-legged sitting position on the cool stone floor, the words of the Sioux medicine man float through my mind, "You are on the right path. Don't stop, keep going." Then Miao's mantric singing fills the cave and my mind goes blank.

Timeless time passes and, surfacing from a deep meditation, I hear Miao's voice seemingly far away, "Loving Tara will now teach us a mudra and a mantra."

I smile thinking of the first time she said those words. We've come a long way since the Mill Valley Community Center. As the *I Ching* taught me all those years ago, all our lives are in a state of constant change, a fluid, ongoing creation. Looking around the cave where spiritual masters have meditated and taught for thousands of years, I fill myself with the energy of ancient wisdom. My heart is full of love as we chant, "*Namo Zhun Ti So Ha*," and, resting in the echoing vibration, I feel certain that even if there are times when we have little money, the final answer to my son's question is, "No, we will never be poor."

* * *

"Blue Pearl, Blue Pearl, from Divine blessing, most precious jewel, Blue Pearl, Blue Pearl, deep in my heart, most precious jewel."

Om Mani Padme Hum

Mitakuye, Oyasi.

As it was in the beginning, is now and ever shall be, world without end.

Afterword

I offer my story as a memoir: my personal journey of learning an entirely new way to not only live, but also to find joy in a world in which the unexpected happens, impermanence rules, and things we thought would last forever, inevitably don't. Cancer was my wake up call, but it is my hope and belief that what I've learned might help anyone faced with loss and the need to let go of the old if we want something new to arise.

I'm now a cancer survivor with a story, but mine is only one of many stories. The American Cancer Society anticipates that 1,638,910 people will be diagnosed with cancer in 2012. About 577,190 Americans are expected to die of cancer in 2012—about 1,500 people a day. I fully respect each person's individual choices about how to respond to their disease.

I was shocked when a friend who read my book said, "So would you tell people to not do chemotherapy?"

My message is that we have a full array of healing practices available to us from both Western and Eastern traditions. My choice has been to blend them into a combined approach that addresses not only my physical body, but my emotional, mental and spiritual terrain as well.

My view is that by the time cancer has manifested as a disease process in the physical body, it is important to take advantage of all Western medicine has to offer. In my case, that was a powerful chemotherapy regimen. As far as I know, there is currently no alternative approach that by itself can cure the physical disease once it has taken hold. Certainly there may be advanced yogis who have such powers, but most of us have not yet evolved to the point of on-demand access to such advanced abilities.

But to only avail our selves of these Western protocols, aimed solely at eradicating what I believe to be the physical symptom of a complex disease process that actually involves body, mind and spirit, seems short sighted. The studies are quite clear that we all have pre-cancerous micro-tumors in our bodies, but if all is working well, our immune system keeps them in check. Cancer only manifests as a disease process if there is a hospitable environment for it, an environment that includes mental, emotional, and spiritual, as well as physical processes. It is this environment that we can influence by Eastern practices passed down over thousands of years through ancient lineages.

Through the wonderful work of Jon Kabat-Zinn, mindfulness meditation has become a mainstay of the burgeoning field of Mind/Body Medicine. But I believe this is only the tip of the iceberg in terms of the powerful healing practices available to us from Eastern traditions.

My good fortune was to meet Yuan Miao after Guan Shi Yin directed her to leave China and travel to the United States. The message given to her was, "The apex of human civilization is created upon the merging of Eastern and Western cultures." She generously teaches practices and ways of viewing the world that in the past would have been considered esoteric secrets, only passed down to select lineage recipients. There is now a belief by many Eastern masters that the need in the world to alleviate suffering is so great that these secrets must be shared more universally.

In addition to meditation practices, the mudras, mantras, powerful visualizations, breathing and movement exercises, and her Yoga of Joy help us quiet the mind and create harmony throughout our entire being. Like mindfulness meditation they have beneficial effects on the physical body, while also helping us to manage emotions and connect to a higher state of consciousness.

I believe these practices have been instrumental in helping me heal from cancer. When I say this I am not only talking about reducing tumor load in my body. The chemotherapy obviously focused on eliminating the tumors, which were growing in an aggressive way with potential to damage other organs and monopolize vital resources necessary for life of the whole system.

But chemotherapy offered nothing to help me manage an array of challenging emotions related to receiving a cancer diagnosis, anticipating treatment, and actually undergoing the chemotherapy, to say nothing of healing (and not worsening) the internal terrain that had provided a supportive environment for the cancer to develop in the first place. Miao's practices empowered me to create a state of internal peace and harmony, which also helped my physical body to optimally utilize the Western treatments.

By the end of the chemotherapy treatment, I had not only eliminated physical tumors, I had developed daily practices and new ways of thinking that help me continue to accept impermanence, pacify anger, minimize stress, eliminate sadness, maintain equanimity, achieve harmony and balance, and find peace and joy even in a world in which we can't control everything that happens. It is my firm belief that this is what is helping me to heal on all levels, emotionally, mentally, spiritually, and then ultimately physically. Learning how to create a healthy internal terrain may help people not develop a disease like cancer in the first place.

I have now been in complete remission for five years. I am grateful every day to have my life. I am still shedding old skins and feeling amazed that I have somehow become part of the older generation. I continue to do the practices every day and one of my greatest joys is teaching them to others.

Surviving cancer has been a significant miracle in my life, but the miracles continue to happen. One of my greatest challenges has been to let go of control and trust more. Miao will often say to us, "One hundred percent—no doubt!" I think by this she means to trust our selves, but not our "little selves."

Lately she stresses, "You are so much bigger than your self." This becomes a kind of koan for me—stretching my mind to think of what we are beyond our usual concepts. I also think she means that doubt holds us back, causing us to constrict out of fear. Her encouragement is to have courage, stay on your path, and not let obstacles defeat you. I'm thinking back to the Jesse Colin Young song my son sang at the Summer of Love party, "Fear's the way we die."

After the chemotherapy I knew I could not go back to my old way of working if I wanted to stay alive. But that way was tried and true: I knew I could generate a good income doing it the old way. I had tremendous fear of trying to change, and the attempt was decimating our savings. One of my biggest fears was that this would mean we could no longer financially support our son to attend college. I kept trying to stay on the new path: "One hundred percent—no doubt."

My son also forged ahead with his own version of no doubt. An excellent student, he set his sights high, applying to competitive (and expensive) schools. Remembering my father and the Bank Night raffle that sent him to medical school, I fought back my fears of crushing disappointment for Toby if he were accepted to schools we couldn't afford. April first is the day of reckoning for college applicants; through some weird quirk of fate, acceptances and rejections arrive on April Fools Day.

Standing in a shaft of sunlight, blond hair glowing, he opened the envelope from Stanford University. "We are happy to inform you of your acceptance into the class of 2012. You have been awarded a full tuition scholarship for all four years. Welcome to Stanford."

One hundred percent—no doubt. Miracles happen. Fear's the way we die.

Acknowledgments

First and foremost I want to express my deep gratitude to my teacher, Yuan Miao, for generously sharing her great wisdom, compassion and joyful spirit. She has been my guiding light, showing me the way home again and again to the healing source that is within us all. Her belief in me has given me courage and inspired me to keep going even when I have doubted myself.

I want to honor my parents, Theodore H. and Isabel R. Sattler, for the model and foundation they provided of love, generosity, a sense of adventure and curiosity, and respect for all beings. I am grateful for the high expectations they had for me, and for their unfailing belief that I could meet them.

My ancestors on both sides of my family courageously blazed trails before me, learning lessons and gaining wisdom that have eventually supported me on my journey. I bow down to Yeshe Tsuomo, Miao's grandma, for her great wisdom, and all she imparted to Miao. Those of us who have been graced with knowing Miao have benefited greatly.

This book would never have been completed without the steadfast support of my husband, Gary. He has believed in me and in the message of the book since its inception, and even when I have wavered in my resolve, he has not. He has been steady like a mountain—participating in literal years of late night spiritual discussions, editing and re-editing, providing all of the technical and artistic expertise needed—creating the layout, cover design, and illustrations with love and devotion that shine from the pages. His big heart has remained reliably open, and it has been my constant source of refuge and renewal.

I will always be grateful for the wisdom and compassion of JoAnn Whittington who guided me through years of both joy and struggle, first as my therapist and then as consultant for my psychotherapy practice. She was my anchor when the ground seemed to be shifting underneath me, helping me learn to trust myself and to understand that the universe can be a place of abundance.

My fellow spiritual seeker and friend, David Holland, spent many long hours editing multiple drafts, helping me sort out tangled spiritual questions, and using his sharp wit and sense of humor to prevent me from taking myself too seriously. For this we should all be grateful!

My sister Ann, niece Meredith, nephew Andy, and I are all part of the same lineage. To them I am deeply grateful for their love and generosity, which reminded me of the strong shoulders on which we all stand. My son, Toby, by his very being, reminded me to keep looking at life with a fresh perspective.

I thank Dwight McKee for expressing his delight in the book – his story of being so absorbed in the story that he forgot his computer on an airplane, was a touchstone for me when I began to lose perspective. I am also grateful for his medical expertise and willingness to write the foreword as both a scientist and spiritual seeker.

Peggy Koop buoyed my spirits by her generous and openhearted offerings of the book's impact on her, which seemed to arrive by email at just the times I most needed them.

I offer armloads of flowers to all my early readers who were so kind and patient and generous with their time and comments: Yicheng Chen, Colleen Craig, Judy Quail Iacuzzi, Trisha Kelly, Peggy Koop, Aishu Lo, Walter Lo, Jill McKee, Ann Sattler Walker, Marina Spence, and Fay Wang.

I especially want to thank Lisa Oz for her generosity of time and spirit in not only reading an early draft, but in offering specific feedback for revision.

My editor, Susan Dalsimer, consistently demonstrated sensitivity to my story, belief in the book and an ability to understand both what needed to be expanded and what needed to be left out.

To all those who created and continue to nurture the Blue Pearl Group, I will be forever grateful for the many opportunities you created, allowing us to be in the presence of our beautiful teacher.

This book would not have been possible without the love and support of The New Century Foundation International. Their commitment to uniting the wisdom, knowledge and spirit of the East and West for the purpose of enhancing the total wellness of individuals from all walks of life has been my constant source of inspiration.

CPSIA information can be obtained at www.ICGtesting.com
Printed in the USA
LVOW051925020613

336548LV00001B/185/P

9 780615 706351